# COMMUNITY RESOURCES AND LEGISLATION

## CYW 103

### PRELIMINARY EDITION

NANCY RUSSELL
CHRISTINE GOODWIN-DE FARIA
*Humber College*

**Kendall Hunt**
publishing company

www.kendallhunt.com
*Send all inquiries to:*
4050 Westmark Drive
Dubuque, IA 52004-1840

Printed in the United States of America
10  9  8  7  6  5  4  3

# CONTENTS

## UNIT 1

### GOVERNMENT, ADVOCACY, COMMUNITY RESOURCES, HISTORY OF SOCIAL SERVICES, CHILD AND YOUTH CARE PROFESSION ..................... 1

# UNIT 2

## THE CHILD AND FAMILY SERVICES ACT (CFSA)

# UNIT 3

## YOUTH CRIMINAL JUSTICE ACT (YCJA)

# UNIT 4

## THE EDUCATION ACT ............................................................................ 63

# ACKNOWLEDGMENTS

The authors would like to thank Pam Howard for her initial contribution to the classroom handbook for this course. This handbook has evolved and expanded over the years in order to meet the increasing and ever-changing demands of relevancy, the need for updated information as well as the growing reliance on Internet-based links and connections.

# UNIT 1

## GOVERNMENT, ADVOCACY, COMMUNITY RESOURCES, HISTORY OF SOCIAL SERVICES, CHILD AND YOUTH CARE PROFESSION

## INTRODUCTION

"Government" impacts our everyday lives in many ways. How long do children attend school? How much do you pay for postsecondary education? How does transportation work in your city? Is the quality of the food you buy protected? How much tax do you pay? How are agencies that care for children funded? How can we be sure that all caregivers implement the residential standards for children in care?

Understanding government and how government "works" is an important component of your role as a child and youth worker (CYW). Accessing resources, using your knowledge of the legislation to help others and sometimes using the legislation to move agencies forward to implement fair practices are just some examples of how this knowledge can be useful in the field. Understanding a rights-based approach and genuinely engaging with children and youth to make a difference in their lives is part of good child care practice.

There are important reasons that you need to know the material in the *Community Resources and Legislation Course*:

- Protects you and your employer from liability.
- Protects the children and youth you work with from "harm" that you might inadvertently cause by not knowing or following laws, policies, procedures, etc. You are an agent of help and of change, many children and youth have been damaged and mistreated by the "system" that as a CYW you want to do everything possible to prevent any more harm being done.
- At times you will be the "voice" for the children and youth you serve; you become an advocate and in your role as advocate, it is your business to be as informed as possible in order that you can give the best help at all times.

- At times you are the interpreter and the translator. Rights and legislation can be confusing for children to understand. The referral process and waitlists for community resources can be difficult to maneuver. Don't assume that child welfare workers, probation officers, and lawyers are always totally informed with the most updated information. Sometimes even if they have the best information it may not be passed on in a way that can be completely understood. In order for you to explain the information with clarity and relevance it is important that you fully understand it.
- Having this knowledge provides consistency in the field for children, youth, and families.
- Having this knowledge and resources also helps to guide the child and youth worker through the right steps to deal appropriately with issues and situations that arise.
- Knowledge helps to empower children and youth. Knowledge helps to elevate the voice of children and youth.
- Knowledge is power.

# FEDERAL GOVERNMENT

Canada's Constitution establishes parliament's authority and sets out its powers for making laws. Canada functions as a federal state. This means that it brings together a number of political communities with a common government for common purposes (**federal**) and separate "state" or "provincial" governments for special purposes of each community (**provincial or municipal**).

The federal government has the exclusive right to create criminal law for the entire nation. The Criminal Code of Canada and the Youth Criminal Justice Act are examples of federal acts.

The federal government is also responsible for National Defense, Currency, the Income Tax Act, the Immigration Act, the Narcotics Control Act, Human Rights and Freedoms, and the Royal Mounted Police among others.

Elected representatives are called Members of Parliament (MPs). Mandatory elections take place every five years.

Canada's federal government is housed on 'Parliament Hill' in Ottawa, Ontario, and is in fact called "Parliament."

Canada's governmental system is divided into three branches: the legislative branch or Parliament, which makes Canada's laws; the executive branch; and the judicial branch. The legislative branch consists of the Queen (with the Governor General as the Queen's representative), the Senate, and the House of Commons. The executive branch consists of the Governor General, acting by and on the advice of the Prime Minister and the Cabinet to implement the laws. The judicial branch interprets and applies the laws. It is made up of the Supreme Court of Canada, the Federal Court of Canada, and the Provincial Courts. The judicial branch is entirely independent of the other two branches of government.

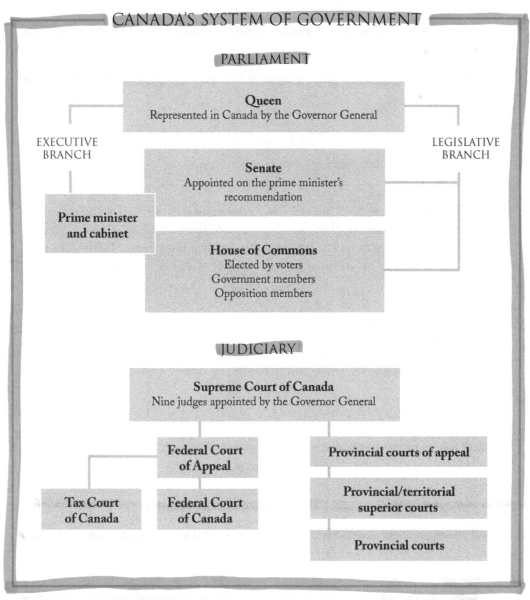

## CANADA'S SYSTEM OF GOVERNMENT

### PARLIAMENT

**Queen**
Represented in Canada by the Governor General

EXECUTIVE
BRANCH

LEGISLATIVE
BRANCH

**Senate**
Appointed on the prime minister's
recommendation

**Prime minister
and cabinet**

**House of Commons**
Elected by voters
Government members
Opposition members

### JUDICIARY

**Supreme Court of Canada**
Nine judges appointed by the Governor General

**Federal Court
of Appeal**

**Provincial courts of appeal**

**Tax Court
of Canada**

**Federal Court
of Canada**

**Provincial/territorial
superior courts**

**Provincial courts**

*Forsey, E. A. (n.d.). How Canadians Govern Themselves: 7th Edition. Retrieved from
http://www2.parl.gc.ca/Sites/LOP/AboutParliament/Forsey/index-e.asp*

## CANADIAN PARLIAMENT

Canadian Parliament is composed of the Queen and two chambers of Parliament called the Senate and the House of Commons.

The two key features of Canadian Parliament are Representative and Responsible Government.

**Responsible Government:** The notion that governments are *accountable* to the *whole* population of the country.

**Representative Government:** *Equal* representation of the *geographical regions* of Canada based loosely on *population*.

## THE BROADER CONTEXT OF PARLIAMENT

Parliament is a legislative body that functions as an instrument of government within a broader structure that includes the Executive Branch and the Judicial Branch.

In the Westminster-based model of parliamentary government, the Executive, composed of the Prime Minister and the Cabinet, is incorporated into Parliament, while retaining a separate sphere of authority and autonomy. The Judiciary, consisting of the Supreme Court and all other courts of the land, is the third branch of government that is also independent of either Parliament or the Executive.

### Queen

The roots of Canada's parliament lie in Britain with the Queen being the formal head of state. The British North America Act, which was developed by British Parliament, created the Canadian Parliament.

No bill can pass into law without the Royal Assent of the Queen or her representative who is the Governor General.

### Composition

*Governor General*—Queen's representative appointed on the advice of the Prime Minister.

*Prime Minister*—Leader of the political Party with the most seats in the House of Commons.

*Parliament*—
   a) *Senate*—members appointed by the Governor General.
   b) *House of Commons*—members elected by Canadian people. Cabinet selected by Prime Minister to head departments of the government.

## House of Commons, 40th Parliament Distribution of Seats, by Political Party

| PROVINCE | Conserv. | Liberal | B.Q. | N.D.P. | Ind. | Vacant | Total |
|---|---|---|---|---|---|---|---|
| Newfoundland and Labrador | | 6 | | 1 | | | 7 |
| Prince Edward Island | 1 | 3 | | | | | 4 |
| Nova Scotia | 4 | 5 | | 2 | | | 11 |
| New Brunswick | 6 | 3 | | 1 | | | 10 |
| Quebec | 11 | 14 | 48 | 1 | 1 | | 75 |
| Ontario | 50 | 37 | | 17 | 1 | 1 | 106 |
| Manitoba | 9 | 1 | | 3 | | 1 | 14 |
| Saskatchewan | 13 | 1 | | | | | 14 |
| Alberta | 27 | | | 1 | | | 28 |
| British Columbia | 22 | 5 | | 9 | | | 36 |
| Yukon Territory | | 1 | | | | | 1 |
| Northwest Territories | | | | 1 | | | 1 |
| Nunavut | 1 | | | | | | 1 |
| TOTAL | 144 | 76 | 48 | 36 | 2 | 2 | 308 |

NOTE: IN 2003, ONTARIO, ALBERTA, AND BRITISH COLUMBIA ALL INCREASED THE NUMBER OF SEATS OFFICIALLY ALLOTTED IN THEIR REGIONS. ONTARIO ADDED THREE SEATS, ALBERTA AND BRITISH COLUMBIA EACH ADDED TWO SEATS. THE NUMBER OF SEATS ALLOCATED TO EACH PARTY CHANGES WITH ELECTIONS.

## Senate

The Governor General on advice from the Prime Minister appoints the 105 members of the Senate. They provide regional representation from across all of Canada. There is no specified length of time a person can remain in the Senate as they are appointed, not elected. Senators hold office until the age of 75 unless they miss two consecutive sessions of Parliament.

The Senate examines legislation introduced by the House of Commons. They may also initiate their own bills, have a diplomatic role, or be involved in research.

The Senate has all of the powers of the House of Commons except that of initiating financial legislation.

## House of Commons

The Canadian people in a national election elect all members of the House of Commons. Members are responsible for most of the legislation introduced into parliament. Critical issues are debated and members speak on behalf of all Canadians.

*Cabinet* is an executive council of ministers with specific duties who have been selected by the Prime Minister from the members elected to the House of Commons.

The party with the most elected members normally forms the government to run the affairs of the nation. The party with the second most members is the official opposition.

There are 308 seats in the House of Commons.

The Speaker of the House of Commons is elected by secret ballot by the members of the House after each general election. The Speaker functions as the presiding officer and is expected to be non-partisan and impartial.

## THE JUDICIAL BRANCH

The "judicial branch" of government is known as the third branch or also as the Supreme Court of Canada. This is an *independent* branch of government.

The *rule of law* means that no one is above the law… not the government, Prime Minister, or the Queen.

The Supreme Court is the highest court in the land. It is composed of nine judges, three of whom must come from Quebec. Judges of the Supreme Court are appointed by the Governor General on the advice of Cabinet and hold office until they reach 75 years old. The court makes final decisions on the interpretation of law based on the Canadian constitution.

## Hansard

Hansard, also titled the Official Report of Debates, is essentially a verbatim transcript of the proceedings in the Senate and the House of Commons. Hansard is published after each sitting day and can be found on the Internet at http://www.parl.gc.ca.

# PROVINCIAL GOVERNMENT

Each province within Canada was given the authority to create its own government under the Constitution Act of 1867.

The provincial government creates and enforces Regulatory Laws of a civil nature and enforces Federal Criminal Law within provincial boundaries.

The provincial government is also responsible for the Provincial Offences Act, Child and Family Services Act, Highway Traffic Act, and Education Act, among others.

Elected representatives are called Members of Provincial Parliament (MPPs). Mandatory elections are held every four years.

Ontario's provincial government is housed in "Queens Park" in Toronto, Ontario.

The Queen is represented by the Lieutenant Governor who is appointed by the Governor General on the advice of the Prime Minister.

## LEGISLATIVE ASSEMBLY

This is a one-house system composed of 125 members elected by the people of Ontario.

There is no Senate in the provincial government, however, there is a cabinet composed of elected members chosen by the Premier to head government departments.

### *Composition*

*Lieutenant Governor*—appointed by Governor General on advice of the Prime Minister.

*Premier*—leader of party with most members elected.

# MUNICIPAL GOVERNMENT

Municipal government is responsible for matters that affect the local area. For example, garbage collection, bus services, libraries, school boards, and emergency services (police, fire, ambulance).

There are 832 municipalities in Ontario with the largest being Toronto containing over two million residents and Cockburn Island being the smallest with only three permanent residents.

A local municipality may be called a city, a town, township, or village depending on its size.

A municipal council whose members are called aldermen or councillors governs our local areas.

In a city or town, the head of council is called a *Mayor* while a *Reeve* is the head of council in villages and some townships.

Local elections are held every three years, always on the second Monday in November throughout the entire province.

*By-Laws* are laws that are made and govern only that municipality. The provincial government limits the things that a municipality may do and council can pass by-laws only on matters that are allowed by the province.

## School Boards

The province's Ministry of Education sets general policies and standards for all school boards. Within those guidelines the local school boards, elected by the residents, decide how best to meet the needs of their students. Thus, school trustees are elected during municipal elections.

School board members are called *Trustees* and are responsible for building and maintaining schools, hiring teachers and staff, and approving programs and textbooks.

On January 1, 1998, 72 district school boards were established in Ontario, replacing 129 school boards. At the same time, 37 smaller, geographically isolated boards and hospital school boards were renamed "school authorities."

## The Municipal Clerk's Office

It is the clerk's job to know which municipal departments or employees do what and where they can be reached. Call the clerk if you require assistance.

In Toronto, *The City Clerk's Office* oversees and manages decision-making processes and related activities for Toronto City Council, Community Councils, Council Standing Committees, and task forces of Council. City Clerk's Office staff provides office support for the Office of the Mayor and Councillors' offices.

## Civil Law

*Civil law* involves laws dealing with the rights of citizens that are based on statutes or legal principles. The modern system is based upon Roman law. Most European countries follow the *civil law* system. The only province in Canada that follows the *civil law* system is Quebec. Modern countries that do not adhere to *civil law* (for the most part) were colonized by England and apply the system of *common law* prevailing there.

## COMMON LAW/CASE LAW

*Common law* or *case law* incorporates a system of laws that are based on judges' decisions and case precedents over time rather than statutes.

## BIJURAL

Canada is considered a *bijural* state or country. A system is called *bijural* when two legal traditions coexist within a single state or country. Canada is *bijural* because common law and civil law coexist in both official languages.

*Note: The charts on pages 10 and 11 are to be read from the bottom of the page up.

## HOW FEDERAL STATUTES ARE CREATED

*A statute is an Act passed by the entire governing body*

### The Passage of a Federal Bill

Proclaimed in Legislature

Governor General

(Signs)

(Royal Assent)

| SENATE | HOUSE OF COMMONS |
|---|---|
| 3$^{rd}$ Reading | 3$^{rd}$ Reading |
| (A formality) | (A formality) |
| | |
| Committee for Study | To Committee |
| | (Clause-by-clause examination) |
| | |
| 2$^{nd}$ Reading | 2$^{nd}$ Reading |
| | (Debate, amendments, if any, speeches) |
| | Vote |
| | |
| 1$^{st}$ Reading | 1$^{st}$ Reading |
| | (A formality) |
| | (Minister introduces proposal) |

**CABINET**

(Creates the "Bills")

## HOW PROVINCIAL STATUTES ARE CREATED

### *The Passage of a Provincial Bill*

Proclaimed in Legislature

LIEUTENANT GOVERNOR

(Signs)

Royal Assent

3$^{rd}$ Reading

(A formality)

**Vote**

**TO COMMITTEE**

For study

Clause-by-Clause Examination

2$^{nd}$ Reading

Debate, Amendments if any, Speeches, Vote

1$^{st}$ Reading

(A formality)

CABINET

Creates

The "Bills"

## WANT MORE INFO?

- *Canadian Parliament*: www.parl.gc.ca
- *Canadian Parliament* Toll Free Line: 1-800-267-7362
- *Governor General of Canada:* The official website of the Governor General. http://www.gg.ca/index.aspx
- *Elections Canada* is an independent, non-partisan agency that reports directly to Parliament. www.elections.ca/home
- *Ontario Provincial Government*: http://www.gov.on.ca/
- *Ontario Provincial Government* Toll Free Line: 1-800-267-8097
- *Legislative Assembly of Ontario:* The official website of the Ontario Legislature. http://www.ontla.on.ca/web/home.do
- *Elections Ontario* is a non-partisan Agency of the Legislative Assembly of Ontario. The Agency works under the direction of the Chief Electoral Officer, an officer of the Legislative Assembly. http://www.elections.on.ca/en-CA/
- *Association of Municipalities of Ontario*: www.yourlocalgovernment.com/ylg/ontario.html
- *City of Toronto website:* The official website about Toronto's municipal government.    http://www.toronto.ca/city_hall/index.htm
- *Department of Justice Canada – Justice Laws Website* is an online source of the consolidated Acts and regulations of Canada. http://laws.justice.gc.ca/en/
- *e-Laws* is a database of Ontario's statutes and regulations, both consolidated and source law. http://www.e-laws.gov.on.ca
- *Canadian Legal Information Institute (CanLII)* is a non-profit organization managed by the Federation of Law Societies of Canada. CanLII's goal is to make Canadian law accessible for free on the Internet. http://www.canlii.org
- *Statistics Canada* produces statistics that help Canadians better understand their country— its population, resources, economy, society, and culture. In Canada, providing statistics is a federal responsibility. As Canada's central statistical agency, Statistics Canada is legislated to serve this function for the whole of Canada and each of the provinces and territories. http://www.statcan.gc.ca/
- *"How'd They Vote"* website: A website that helps you to find any MP and see their voting history, attendance, and speaking habits. http://howdtheyvote.ca
- *Student Vote* is a non-profit educational initiative working to inspire the habit of electoral and community participation among students across Canada. www.studentvote.ca
- *Apathy is Boring* uses art and technology to educate youth about democracy. www.apathyisboring.com
- *The Foundation for the Study of Processes of Government in Canada* is a not-for-profit organization that promotes understanding of the role and function of the three levels of government in Canada and the meaning of Canadian citizenship. www.igloo.org/forum

## DEFINITIONS

ACT – A bill, which has been passed through the various legislative steps required for it and become law. Also an Act of Parliament is a Bill that has been passed by Parliament.

AGENDA – A list of the items of business to be dealt with during a sitting of the House or of one of its committees.

ALDERMEN or COUNCILLORS – The members of a municipal council (government).

AMENDMENT – The correction or alteration of a law, Bill, or Act. Example: Bill 82 was proposed to amend the Education Act.

BILL – A proposed law presented to a lawmaking body for examination, possible amendment or approval. In Canada this means it must receive a majority vote in Parliament. When passed they cease to remain Bills and become law (e.g., Bill 77 became the Child and Family Services Act). Bills that are first introduced in the Senate are prefixed with the letter "S." Bills originating in the House of Commons are prefixed with the letter "C."

BY-LAW – Laws that are in effect only in that municipality. The provincial government limits the things that a municipality may do and council can pass by-laws only on matters that are allowed in the province.

CABINET – The executive of the government, consisting of those Members and Senators appointed by the Governor General on the advice of the Prime Minister. Formally a committee of the Privy Council, it is responsible for the administration of the government and the establishment of its policy.

CHAIR – The presiding officer at a meeting of the House or a committee.

COMING-INTO-FORCE-CLAUSE – The clause of a bill stating the date upon which an Act will come into effect.

CONSTITUENCY – The specific geographic area in Canada that a Member of Parliament represents in the House of Commons, also known as a riding or electoral district.

COUNTY – An area created by territorial division for the purpose of local government.

DEBATE – A discussion in which the arguments for and against a subject are presented according to specific rules.

DISSOLUTION – The bringing to an end of a Parliament, either at the conclusion of its five-year term or by proclamation of the Governor General. It is followed by a general election.

DISTRICT – A division of an area, as for administrative purposes, i.e., school district.

FEDERAL LEGISLATION – Legislation that applies to every part of the country and must be implemented in every province – at least in "spirit" as the basic meaning of the law must not change.

INDEPENDENT MEMBER – A Member who is not a member of a recognized political party. A Member may be elected as an independent or may leave or be expelled from a party during a Parliament and sit as an independent.

LAW – Rules established by a governing authority to institute and maintain orderly coexistence. Any rule of conduct, which can and is, enforced by the courts.

LEGISLATION – The making of laws and the laws made are called legislation.

LIABILITY – Responsibility. Accountability. Obligation under the law.

LOBBY – (1) Rooms adjacent to the government and opposition sides of the Chamber. (2) A group organized for the purpose of influencing the opinions and decisions of legislators with respect to some specific area of interest.

PARLIAMENTARY INTERN – One of a group of ten university graduates selected each year to work as researchers and assistants in the offices of Members. The Canadian Political Science Association sponsors the internship program.

PMO – An abbreviation for Prime Minister's Office.

PORTFOLIO – The term used to describe the responsibilities of a member of Cabinet.

PROCLAMATION – Announcing in the legislature that an Act is Law. Must go through a series of steps to be proclaimed the last one being Royal Assent (the actual signing by the Governor General).

PROROGATION – The ending of a session of Parliament. Prorogation also refers to the period of time a Parliament stands prorogued.

PROVINCIAL LEGISLATION – Laws that pertain only to a specific province. Each province has its own legislation for education, child welfare, family laws, etc.

REGION – A part or section of a country or the world.

REGULATION – A law that is created to implement the Act or Statute. The meeting of legal licensing standards. A rule or order prescribed for government.

RIGHT HONOURABLE – A title given for life to Governors General, Prime Ministers and Chief Justices of the Supreme Court of Canada.

ROYAL ASSENT – The approval, by a representative of the Crown, of a bill passed by the House and the Senate, making it into an Act of Parliament. By tradition, Royal Assent is accorded in the Senate Chamber, usually by a deputy of the Governor General in the presence of Members of the House and Senate. Alternatively, it may be signified by a written declaration, either by the Governor General or her/his deputy.

STATUTES – A formal written enactment of a legislative body. The collection of laws passed by a legislative body.

TABLE – To place a document before the Senate, the House of Commons, or a committee for consideration or consultation.

WELFARE – Well-doing or well-being in any respect; the enjoyment of health and the common blessings of life; exemption from any evil or calamity; prosperity; happiness. Organized efforts by a community or organization to improve the social and economic conditions of a group or class.

WHIP – The Member who is responsible for keeping other members of the same party informed about House business and ensuring their attendance in the Chamber, especially when a vote is anticipated. They also arrange the order of speakers in the legislature, facilitating the Speaker's job.

WITNESS – A person invited to appear before a committee to present an opinion on a particular topic or to provide technical advice with respect to a bill.

# ADVOCACY

Rights-based law and legislation protects children and youth in government care. Provincial, federal, and international law encompasses child and youth rights at all levels. For example, all children in care in Ontario have the right to receive medical and dental care, reasonable privacy, and to speak privately with The Office of the Provincial Advocate for Children and Youth. These rights are enshrined in law and therefore the expectation is that the policies and practices of service providers ensure that the provision of care reflects and respects the law. Children and youth in care are particularly vulnerable and in need of protection.

The Canadian Oxford Dictionary defines advocacy as "verbal support or argument for a cause, policy, etc." and an advocate as "a person who supports or speaks in favour of another." "Advocacy" within the child and youth care field can be defined as promoting the view or preferences of children and youth. Advocacy seeks to elevate or amplify the voices for children and youth. It is important that advocates have an understanding and knowledge of the relevant policies and legislation in order to be effective help agents. The voices of children and youth often raise concerns from their lived experience that shed light on rights violations and gaps in the implementation of rights-based law. By understanding legislated rights–based requirements advocates have the ability to (metaphorically) walk beside children and youth and hold governments and service providers accountable.

There are different types of advocacy: individual rights–based, systemic or systems, and policy. Individual rights–based advocacy seeks to place the views of children and youth ahead of the "best interest" (adult knows best) perspective. This requires that child advocates begin to work from a rights-based framework using rights offered to children and youth in the United Nations Convention on the Rights of the Child and the Child and Family Services Act, for example. Systems advocacy refers to initiatives within the environment of organizations/community that will influence programs and practices to benefit children and youth. When it is clear that policies and practices in agencies get in the way of the quality of life and development of children and youth, then systemic advocacy is necessary. Policy advocacy generally refers to advocacy tactics, strategies, and initiatives, which target changes to policies and/or legislation. Policy advocacy seeks to assist in the establishment of new policies, to improve existing policies, or to challenge polices that diminish resources for children and youth.

The United Nations Convention on the Rights of the Child (UN-CRC) is the singularly most important piece of international rights law that has been enacted worldwide. The UN-CRC was the first legally binding international mechanism to integrate the full range of human rights—civil, cultural, economic, political, and social rights. In 1989, world leaders decided that children needed a special convention just for them because people under 18 years old often need special care and protection that adults do not. The leaders also wanted to make sure that the world acknowledged that children have human rights too.

The Convention outlines these rights in 54 Articles and two Optional Protocols. It spells out the basic human rights that children everywhere have: the right to survival; to develop to the fullest; to protection from harmful influences, abuse, and exploitation; and to participate fully in family, cultural, and social life. The four core principles of the Convention are non-discrimination; devotion to the best interests of the child; the right to life, survival, and development; and respect for the views of the child. Every right set out in the Convention is key to the human dignity and healthy development of every child. The Convention protects children's rights by setting standards in health care; education; and legal, civil, and social services.

By agreeing to accept the obligations of the Convention (by ratifying or acceding to it), national governments have committed themselves to protecting and ensuring children's rights and they have agreed to hold themselves accountable for this commitment before the international community. Canada played a central role in the drafting and promoting of the UN-CRC and was considered a world leader when the CRC was ratified in December 1991. Many governments have enacted legislation, created systems and put into place a range of creative measures to ensure the protection and realization of the rights of children under the age of 18. Each government must also report back on children's rights in their country.

It is important to note that full implementation of the 54 articles contained in the Convention has not yet taken place in this country. If you wish to read more about the UN-CRC please visit the United Nations website at: http://www.un.org/.

In Ontario, The Office of the Provincial Advocate for Children and Youth reports directly to the Legislature and is mandated to provide an independent voice for children and youth, including children with special needs and First Nations children. The Advocate's Office receives and responds to concerns from children, youth, and families who are seeking or receiving services under the Child and Family Services Act and the Education Act (Provincial and Demonstration Schools). The Provincial Advocate may identify systemic problems involving children, conduct reviews, and provide education and advice on the issue of advocacy and the rights of children. The Office is guided by the principles of the UN Convention on the Rights of the Child and has a strong commitment to youth involvement.

Other laws and regulations relevant to children and youth in Ontario can be found in the federal and provincial laws of Canada. This course manual outlines those deemed most significant to basic child and youth care practice. This manual does not provide an exhaustive list of legislation and students are encouraged to move beyond the manual and to explore and research what is relevant to their field placements and practice.

# COMMUNITY RESOURCES

## WANT MORE INFO?

- *United Nations* is an international organization founded in 1945 after the Second World War by 51 countries committed to maintaining international peace and security, developing friendly relations among nations and promoting social progress, better living standards, and human rights. www.un.org
- *Office of the Provincial Advocate for Children and Youth* serves youth in government care and the margins of government care through individual, systemic, and policy advocacy. www.provincialadvocate.on.ca
- *Children's Rights Information Network* is a global network for children's rights. www.crin.org
- *Human Rights Education Associates* is an international non-governmental organization that supports human rights learning and training. www.hrea.org
- *First Nations Child and Family Caring Society of Canada* is an organization dedicated to the promotion of holistic knowledge and practices that support the sharing of national First Nations communities to love, respect, and nurture First Nations children, young people, families, communities, and nations. www.fncfcs.com
- *The Landon Pearson Resource Centre* was created with a powerful vision: every child in Canada will grow up aware of his or her rights and responsibilities and enabled to exercise them within a receptive and respectful society. www.ottawakids.ca
- *Youth in Care Canada (also known as the National Youth in Care Network)* is an organization driven by youth and alumni from care. *Youth in Care Canada* exists to voice the opinions and concerns of youth in and from care and promote the improvement of services for them. www.youthincare.ca

## THE BLUE BOOK

As a Child and Youth Worker (*CYW*), you will be working predominantly with children, adolescents, and families experiencing and suffering from stress, life problems, abuse, crises, and disabilities in some or many areas of functioning.

To select and access the most suitable resources to assist these clients, we must develop a working knowledge of the various resource systems available in each community as well as the types and criteria of service.

In the process of giving and receiving information and making referrals, we must not only be aware of existing resources, but also how to help the client identify their unmet needs and match the most suitable service to those needs.

Much confusion and anxiety of being referred to a service can be alleviated or lessened by the worker who assesses need, finds a suitable resource, and aids in the follow-up work required.

*The Blue Book* provides professionals and clients with a comprehensive catalogue of services available in Toronto. Most cities or regions throughout Ontario (and Canada) provide a similar catalogue.

*The Blue Book* is updated annually and can be purchased by anyone, through an agency called Community Information Services. Instructions on the use of the book are located in the front of the book.

Most youth serving and social service agencies have copies available for their employees. *The Blue Book* can also be accessed at public libraries. The cost of the book is generally between $59 and $99. Price varies in accordance with the edition required (i.e., front line, professional).

*The Blue Book* is also available online at www.211Toronto.ca and as the tools of technology increasingly become a vital component of child and youth care practice, many CYW's prefer the on-line version of *The Blue Book*.

# SOCIAL WELFARE

## DEFINITION OF SOCIAL WELFARE

Social welfare is about how people, communities, and institutions in a society take action to provide certain minimum standards and certain opportunities. It is generally about helping people facing contingencies.

We should distinguish between public and private social welfare.

**Public social welfare:** Canada is a federal state. This means there are three levels: federal, provincial, and municipal all of which play a role in public social welfare. There are also public non-government agencies, advisory boards, and appeal boards. Not only is government involved, but also parliament, the bureaucracy, and judiciary and political parties, all of which play a role in social welfare, from the formulation of social welfare policy to administration. An example of public social welfare is national health care provided by government.

**Private social welfare:** is provided by non-profit or not-for-profit, and commercial or for-profit firms. Many social agencies or organizations are incorporated as non-profit companies. They receive funds from one of the levels of government, as well as private donations to carry on their work. They may also receive funds through contracts to carry out work on behalf of a private company or government. The United Way of Greater Toronto is an example of a non-profit agency providing social welfare to Canadians.

## HISTORICAL DEVELOPMENT OF SOCIAL WELFARE IN CANADA

### 1600s

The Roman Catholic Church cared for the sick, elderly, and abandoned, however, jail was the only public facility available for those unable to care for themselves. Corporal punishment was an acceptable form of intervention.

### 1700s

Around 1750, private groups established institutions to house the poor and needy. A commonly accepted belief was that the poor were in need of correction and discipline. Behaviour was often corrected through the use of whips, chains, and starvation.

Ontario viewed support for the poor as the responsibility of the private sector and continued to utilize jails.

In 1799, the Orphan Act was established; our first Child Welfare Law. This Act was intended to support and educate fatherless children by "binding the child as an apprentice" with the goal of support from the "work ethic" notion. Clients were called apprentices.

This legislation covered females to the age of 16 and males until the age of 21. No systems had ever been established to ensure adequate care of children was provided.

### 1800s

Public education began around 1816 and ensured that education was provided for all, not just the rich privileged.

Between 1849 and 1888 four new Acts were created that allowed for the development of more specialized services.

The Ontario Municipal Corporations Act increased self-government and opened the door for local authorities to provide relief for the poor. With government financial aid, the first general hospitals and children's institutions were established by voluntary organizations.

The Charity Aid Act gave way to the opening of private institutions to care for orphans or children of the poor and unemployed.

Charitable societies were given legal authority to prevent the maltreatment of apprentices through the Industrial Schools Act.

Local school trustees established residential training schools for children under the age of 14. In addition, adoption and institutional care emerged as alternatives to apprentices.

The Act for the Protection and Reformation of Neglected Children gave the courts the power to make children wards of institutions and charitable organizations. Foster homes were developed with the government providing all costs.

In 1891, J.J. Kelso founded the original Children's Aid Society in Toronto.

*As a point of interest the Society for the Prevention of Cruelty to Animals existed prior to anything for children and therefore, animals were essentially receiving as much, if not more, protection than children.*

## 1900s

In 1902 the Children's Aid Societies became semi-public agencies and were given the legal right to remove children from their homes and supervise their shelters. They were given the status of legal guardians and collected municipal dollars for the maintenance of their wards.

Further provision for the welfare of illegitimate children and their mothers and those children who required adoption followed the development of the Children of Unmarried Parents Act and Adoption Act.

In 1954, under the Child Welfare Act, the provincial government accepted direct responsibility for the delivery of child welfare services. The government increased financing for the societies and developed accountability protocols. This act was revised in 1965 and the current Child and Family Services Act was proclaimed in 1984.

In 1930 the Department of Welfare was established, as the depression created high demand for services of the societies and drained municipal monies. This precipitated a gradual shift with societies still being responsible for the delivery of direct service.

In 1908 the Juvenile Delinquent's Act was proclaimed and amended in 1929. This Act recognized that children needed to be treated differently than adults even when they committed a criminal offence. The J.D.A. governed children committing offences between the ages of 7 and 18.

This Act was redesigned and proclaimed as the Young Offenders Act in 1984 and governed children committing criminal acts between the ages of 12 and 18. Those children under 12 who were breaking the law were to be dealt with by their parents or the Children's Aid Society. In 2003, the Young Offenders Act was replaced by the Youth Criminal Justice Act.

The Education Act in Ontario was proclaimed in 1975 and revised in 1980. The most important amendment took place in 1984 by what is commonly called Bill 82. The passing of Bill 82 meant that all Boards of Education were now mandated to provide special services for exceptional children (e.g., deaf, developmentally challenged, gifted).

# CHILD AND YOUTH CARE PROFESSION

## DESCRIPTION OF CHILD AND YOUTH WORK

### *Child and Youth Care Education Consortium January 1992 and University of Victoria/School of Child and Youth Care*

Professional child and youth care is a unique approach to working with children, youth, and their families. A number of characteristics, taken together, differentiate this professional approach from allied human services disciplines. Although a number of these characteristics are shared with various other disciplines, the particular cluster is unique to child and youth care work:

- *Child and youth care is primarily focused on the growth and development of children and youth*
- *Child and youth care is concerned with the totality of a child's functioning*
- *Child and youth care has developed a model of social competence rather than a pathology-based orientation to child development*
- *Child and youth care is based on (but not restricted to) direct, day-to-day work with child, youth, and their families in their environment*
- *Child and youth care involves the development of therapeutic relationships with children, youth, their families, and other informal or formal helpers*

Child and youth care practice focuses on the infant, child, and adolescent, both typical and with special needs, within the context of the family, the community, and the life span. The developmental-ecological perspective emphasizes the interaction between persons and the physical and social environments, including cultural and political settings.

Professional practitioners promote the optimal development of children, youth, and their families in a variety of settings such as early child care and education, community based child and youth development programs, parent education and family support, school-based programs, community mental health, group homes, residential centres, day and residential treatment, early intervention, home-based care and treatment, psychiatric centres, rehabilitation programs, pediatric health care, and juvenile justice programs.

Child and youth care practice includes skills in assessing client and program needs, designing and implementing programs and planned environments, integrating developmental preventative and therapeutic requirements into the life space, contributing to the development of knowledge and practice, and participating in systems interventions through direct care, supervision, administration, teaching, research, consultation, and advocacy.

## The Essence of Child and Youth Work

*Ferguson and Anglin 1985*

1. The primary focus is on the growth and development of children and youth; the family, organizations, and community are the context.
2. The importance of the totality of child development and functioning: the focus is on living through a portion of the life cycle rather than only looking at one facet (e.g., mental or physical health, education).
3. Utilize a model of social competence (versus pathology) and build on strengths through establishing therapeutic relationships. This is in juxtaposition to the *medical model*.
4. Based on direct day-to-day work with children and youth in their environments (e.g., residence, school, hospital, home, street) and remains grounded in direct care work. *Milieu therapy* is widely utilized. Child and youth care workers have broadened the definition of *milieu therapy* and expanded its practice into schools, homes, and the community.

For information on the CYC Milestones, go to
http://www.oacyc.org; Ontario Association of Child and Youth Counsellors
1–888–367–7193

## CYC MILESTONES

1801 – The first professional CYC, Jean Marc Gaspard Itard, commissioned by French government to work with Victor ("The Wild Boy of Aveyron") starting January 1, 1801. Itard was part of the "Moral Therapy" Movement, which saw a humane approach and milieu as the best way to treat psychological problems (basis of CYC approach).

1850s – Residences for "incorrigible" children and orphans established in Ontario: Kingston, 1857; St. Agatha (near Kitchener-Waterloo), 1858; Toronto, The Boys Home, 1859. Few staff, many children, but treatment considered humane.

1859 – "Young offender" facility started, Upper Canada Reformatory Prison started in Penetanguishene, with boys 9 to 20. Occupational skills a major part of program. Boys actually built the building which is still in use today.

1891–1893 – First laws for the care and protection of children, resulting in the establishment of the Children's Aid Society in Toronto.

1905 – Major step in adapting the physical milieu to aid learning, Maria Montessori adapts furniture, learning "toys," room arrangements, etc. to aid street kids and then developmentally handicapped, in Italy. Translated Itard's reports into Italian.

1917 – First attempt to create an entire therapeutic "colony" or social structure by Makarenko, a Russian teacher-social worker (CYC?) for the roving street gangs left after the Russian Revolution.

1945 – Formal CYC training begins in Europe, the psychoéducateur model, to train workers to help socialize European street kids left homeless after World War II – emphasis on therapeutic activities, normalization, healthy relationships, and milieu.

1950s – Major texts outline the basis of the profession in North America, Bettelheim on therapeutic routines, relationships, milieu (1950); Redl & Wineman (1951, 1957), group dynamics, therapeutic activities, behavior management techniques, life-space interview; Erikson (1950) on stages of psycho-social development and the developmental meaning of disturbed behavior and play.

1957 – First formal CYC training program in North America, The Child Care Worker Program at Thistletown Hospital in Rexdale (Toronto).

1959 – First meeting of the OACYC, then called the Thistletown Association of Child Care Workers, in Rexdale, Ontario.

1967 – First "branch" of the OACYC (CCWAO) formed in Ottawa – beginning of the CCW training program in Colleges of Applied Arts & Technology, at the Provincial Institute of Trades/George – Brown College; a 3-year diploma program that spreads rapidly to 19 colleges in the province, to become the largest integrated system of CYC training in North America.

1968 – "Conference on Professional Practice," the first provincial conference specifically for CYCs, sponsored by the Lions Club for the CCWAO, in November in Toronto.

1969 – Incorporation of the OACYC, as the Child Care Workers' Association of Ontario (CCWAO), letters patent granted by Provincial government, August 1.

1974 – "College of Child Care Work" proposal submitted to provincial government (but not accepted) for a regulatory college that would, among other things make it an offence for anyone other than a trained Child Care Worker to use that term for themselves.

1976 – CCWAO leadership in Ministry of Education DACUM to establish standardized curriculum for Child Care Worker Program in Ontario's community colleges.

1977 – First CCWAO Student Awards given to students from 13 college CCW programs.

1979 – Criteria set for accreditation of Full Members in the CCWAO.

1980s – Major professional developments in Canada:

- First Canadian national CYC conference, held in Victoria BC, 1981

- Journal of Child Care, first issue in 1982

- BA program in CYC started at University of Victoria BC

- First International CYC Conference, held in Vancouver BC, 1985

1983 – CCWAO becomes a founding member of the Council of Canadian Child and Youth Care Associations, the national professional association for CYCs in Canada.

1985 – Final adoption of Code of Ethics for the Association.

1989 – Official changing of name from CCWAO to OACYC, granted through supplementary letters patent, November 3 – approval for a Bachelor level program in CYC in Ontario, at Ryerson Polytechnical University – first Ontario CYC to be killed on the job – Krista Sepp, while working in a group home in Midland, Ontario.

1997 – OACYC co-sponsors first International CYC Conference in Ontario –the "5th International" in June, in Toronto – OACYC first CYC association to offer professional liability insurance to members.

1998 – Beginning of major employers recognizing professional CYC staff:

- Kinark Child and Family Services, makes OACYC membership part of their employment criteria, 1998

- Upper Grand District School Board is the first Board to make OACYC membership a requirement for employment, 1999

- Brant Haldimand Norfolk Catholic District School Board is the first Board to have 100% of their CYC staff with professional credentials, 2001

1999 – With over 600 professional members, OACYC becomes the largest CYC association in North America.

- First OACYC conference exclusively by and for CYCs, called "Heroes Within," to celebrate 40th anniversary of the OACYC, held in Kingston, and attracts almost 400 registrants.

- Use of "CYC (Cert.)" professional designation conditions in place (April 30, 1999) in that all Full Certified members have complete documentation submitted to Provincial Office.

2000 – First time an entire class of CYW students joins the OACYC from St. Lawrence College in Kingston.

2001 – OACYC Web site begun (January 17) www.oacyc.org makes its debut on the World Wide Web – OACYC celebrates 200th Anniversary of the profession with a major Provincial Conference in London, Ontario; recognition of 5 OACYC members with 25-year-plus memberships.

2002 – Professional Development Credits required by all Full Members to maintain their professional membership in the OACYC (January, 2002).

- First OACYC Conference devoted to one sector of the profession, the "School-based CYC Work" Conference at Mohawk College, Brantford.

2003 – First OACYC Conference in northern Ontario "Making a Giant Difference" in Thunder Bay is so successful the program has to be extended from one day to two and a half days to accommodate presentations.

2004 – "CYC" approved as the second professional designation for full professional members (those without a CCW or CYW diploma).

- Official CYC "Scope of Practice" statement adopted by the OACYC:

The practice of Child and Youth Counselling is: "The assessment of maladaptive behavior patterns and social-emotional functioning in children, adolescents, and young adults and the prevention and treatment of conditions in the individual, family, and community, in order to develop, maintain, and promote emotional, social, behavioural, and interpersonal well-being within the context of daily living."

2005 – CYC WEEK permanently moved to first full week in May to coincide with international CYC Week recognition of first CYC Instructor in Ontario, William T. "Lon" Lawson, on the 90th anniversary of his birth.

*Source: © Ontario Association of Child and Youth Counsellors – 2002–2005*

## Ontario Association of Child and Youth Counsellors (OACYC)

The Ontario Association of Child and Youth Counsellors is the professional association representing approximately 1,500 Child and Youth Counsellors (CYCs) in the province of Ontario, Canada. It also provides a voice for the other 8,000 child and youth workers in the province. OACYC:

- Is the largest CYC provincial Association and a founder of the Council of Canadian Child and Youth Care Associations
- Consults with government and social service agencies on youth and CYC issues
- Sponsors scholarships and awards for CYC training programs; also co-sponsors the province-wide Krista Sepp Award for excellence in CYC work
- Represents eight sectors of Child and Youth Work in the province of Ontario - school-based, residential, youth justice, hospitals, children's mental health, child welfare, private practice, educators
- Publishes provincial newsletter, the *Chronicle* and sponsors workshops and national conferences for CYCs
- Provides Professional Liability Insurance for CYCs in private practice

**For more information on the OACYC contact:**

Ontario Association of Child and Youth Counsellors
27 Victoria Street East/Suite 207/PO Box 22/Alliston, ON. L9R 1T7
www.oacyc.org
**TOLL FREE IN ONTARIO**
**1-888-367-7193**

## Major Areas of CYW Employment

The roots of the "Child and Youth Worker" began in residential programs and day care centres. Current practice sees child and youth care counsellors in all of the following areas:

1. Residential day treatment and residential treatment
2. Recreation – Community recreation centres, day camps, residential camps
3. Recreation – Outward Bound programs
4. School support in the classroom
5. School-based youth and family counseling
6. Rehabilitation
7. Hospital
8. Juvenile justice
9. Community-based programs
10. Community outreach
11. Child and youth advocacy
12. Parent education and training, family support
13. Infant development, early childhood care and education
14. Day care
15. Home-based care

# UNIT 2

## THE CHILD AND FAMILY SERVICES ACT (CFSA)

## THE CHILD AND FAMILY SERVICES ACT (CFSA)

The Child and Family Services Act received Royal Assent on December 14, 1984, and was proclaimed in the Legislative Assembly in November 1985.

The CFSA is a Provincial Act that presents a common philosophy for services to children and families and the protection of children in Ontario. It also addresses the large issue of child protection.

The Children's Aid Society (CAS) is established under the authority of the CFSA. Each local CAS is operated by a Board of Directors elected from the local community and by the membership of the CAS at large.

The Act recognizes the importance of family in a child's life. As much as possible, supportive services are offered in the least restrictive fashion. The Act promotes the notion of mutual consent between the parents and Children's Aid Societies.

Children's Aid Societies have been given the right and responsibility to ensure the protection of children in Ontario. In some communities this agency may be called Family and Children's Services. Any agency responsible for the protection of children may be referred to as a "Child Welfare" agency.

The Act covers children from birth to 18 years of age. The CAS will not intervene on behalf of a young person 16 years of age or older if they were not in the care of the CAS prior to turning 16. Young persons are no longer considered "children in need of protection" at that age. If, however, a young person is a ward of the CAS, they may receive services and support up to the age of 18. If they continue in school they will be supported until the age of 21. Such an agreement is called an "extended care and maintenance agreement."

The CFSA takes special provisions and takes special care to address the needs of aboriginal (First Nations) children, youth, and their families. The Act itself outlines its main purpose as well as secondary purposes. These are very important as they give us a context of what the CFSA is all about. The paramount purpose of this Act is to promote the best interests, protection, and well-being of children. The additional purposes of the Act, so long as they are consistent with the best interests, protection, and well-being of children are listed on pages 84-85 of the Appendices section of this handbook.

The last large-scale revision of the CFSA was in 2005. The CFSA is mandated to be revised every five years. The *Report on the 2005 Review of the Child and Family Services Act – Ministry of Children and Youth Services* can be accessed in PDF format via the Internet at www.children.gov. on.ca/CS/en/publications/CFSAReview.htm

The report lists several areas that require reform: adoption, range of options offered to children in care must provide children with a sense of stability, continuity, and permanence. Heritage and culture must be taken into account as well as relationships with family and community, and the scope of power of child welfare agencies must be balanced by empowering children in care with a genuine voice for themselves and their families. A strong recommendation also includes the implementation of a meaningful and responsive complaints procedure.

Bill 210, the *Child and Family Services/Statute Law Amendment Act,* passed in early 2006 by the McGuinty government, is designed to make CASs more accountable to the communities they serve and increase the number of permanency options for children and youth in the care of CAS. More detailed information is available on the Ministry of Children and Youth Services website: www.children.gov.on.ca

When you see a copy of the Act you will notice the letters "R.S.O." stamped on the cover. This stands for Revised Statutes of Ontario. Statutes are collections of laws passed by a legislative body, in this case the Ontario legislature.

## FLEXIBLE SERVICES

The needs of children and families are always changing. The Act allows for flexibility in the funding and delivery of services to meet these changing needs areas.

There are five broad categories of children's services:

1. Child Welfare – residential, nonresidential, prevention, child protection, adoption, and individual or family counselling services
2. Child Treatment – services for children with mental health or psychiatric disorders (and/or their families)

3. Child Development – services for children with developmental or physical handicaps (and/or their families)
4. Community Support – support or prevention services provided in the community for children and their families
5. Young Offenders – services for young persons in conflict with the law

## VOLUNTARY AGREEMENTS

The notion of voluntary services implies that there are either no protection issues or the parent(s) are agreeable to ensuring such issues are dealt with.

Parental consent is required for the voluntary placement of a child under 16 years, although a child 12 years of age and older must agree with the plan for placement.

Children 16 years of age may seek confidential counselling without parental consent. The counsellor, however, must discuss with the child at the earliest opportunity, the desirability of involving the child's parents.

## TEMPORARY CARE AGREEMENT (TCA)

This agreement is made between the parents and the CAS when parents are temporarily unable to care for their children on a short-term basis. There is no court involvement for this type of agreement. This is in keeping with the notion of mutual consent as outlined in the principles of the CFSA.

A child 12 or over must consent to the TCA unless an assessment completed within the last year indicated the child's developmental handicap renders him/her unable to participate.

Temporary care agreements do not apply to children 16 or older.

The legal custody of the child transfers to the CAS during this period. The initial agreement may not exceed 6 months, although it may be extended to a maximum of 12 months. If a family is not ready to have their child return home after 12 months the CAS will seek wardship through the court.

## SPECIAL NEEDS AGREEMENT (SNA)

A Special Needs Agreement can be utilized when the special needs of a child are such that the parent is unable to meet them. The agreement may provide for services in the child's home or for care and custody of the child by a CAS or the Minister of Community and Social Services (in the instance of services provided directly by the Ministry Regional Office). A Special Needs Agreement is not used in the case of abuse or neglect. This was put in place for children with physical, intellectual, and/or developmental disabilities, mental health disorders, medical problems, or those who need specialized services to participate in daily living activities. Parental rights are to be primarily maintained with a special needs agreement.

A 16- or 17-year-old youth who has a special need and requires residential and/or other services of a CAS or another agency may also enter into a Special Needs Agreement with a CAS or the Minister. Youth who have left the family home for self-protection, have been abandoned by the parent(s), or whose parent(s) have refused to provide support can negotiate a Special Needs Agreement directly with a CAS. The agreement may have an initial term of up to one year, with a possible extension of up to one additional year.

However, there has been a developing crisis for families of children with special needs in relation to their relationship with Children's Aid Societies and government funding programs.

The question seems to be whether loving and capable parents of children who have severe disabilities are being forced to place them in custody of Children's Aid Societies as "children in need of protection," in order for them to obtain necessary care, and whether there are any possible justifications for such a process. Both within the legislative framework of the CFSA and in the bureaucratic response to the pleas of parents after that framework was essentially abandoned in 1997, many parents have been left with no recourse but to allow themselves to be identified as inadequate, neglectful caregivers for their own children in order to obtain supports through the legislated child-protection authority of the CAS. That authority can only be exercised when legal custody is relinquished by the parents, first temporarily and then permanently. Special Needs Agreements have not been abolished. They are still contemplated by Section 30 of the CFSA. However, the government stopped providing funds to CAS for such arrangements in 1997 and directed societies to use their resources for child protection matters instead.

In May 2005, the Ontario Ombudsman released a 44-page report regarding the issue, entitled *Between a Rock and a Hard Place* and to date the Minister of Children and Youth has responded with both a verbal and financial commitment to implement several of the report's recommendations. Updated reports regarding progress were unavailable at the time of printing.

# COURT ORDERS

## SUPERVISION ORDER

Under a Supervision Order the child is placed, remains with, or is returned to the parent or a relative or other member of the child's community under the supervision of a CAS. The court may specify terms and conditions regarding the child's care and supervision to the guardian, the child, the CAS or other party to the court proceeding. The duration of a Supervision Order is from 3 to 12 months and may be extended indefinitely.

This gives the CAS the right to monitor the family on an ongoing basis with regard to the terms and conditions within the order set out by the court.

Violations of these terms and conditions may deem the child in need of protection and the child/children may be taken into the care of the CAS.

## WARDSHIP

1. Society Wardship – The care and custody of the child is given to the CAS through the courts on a *temporary* basis. Parental rights rest with the CAS.
2. Crown Warship – The care and custody of the child is given to the CAS through the courts on a *permanent* basis. Parental rights rest with the CAS.

**Note:** A child can be in the care of the CAS for a maximum of 12 months if under 6 years of age and 24 months if over 6 years of age before becoming a Crown Ward. The clock begins to tick with either a temporary care agreement or society wardship. If a child returns home at any time the amount of time in care is still counted toward the 24- or 12-month maximum total.

# CONFIDENTIALITY

Parents and children over the age of 12 have the right to see their complete file kept by any social service agency. Once the request has been made the agency has 30 days to respond by releasing information. If any information is withheld, a full explanation must be provided.

Information may be denied for the following reasons:

1. The child is under 16 and the information could cause physical or emotional harm
2. The name of another person contained in the record could cause physical or emotional harm to that person
3. Medical, emotional, developmental, psychological, educational, or social assessments if the content could be misunderstood without appropriate explanation being provided
4. Records for a child over the age of 12 receiving counselling without parental consent can only be shared with parents if the child gives permission
5. Parents may have certain information restricted from their child if the child is under 16 years of age

# CHILDREN'S RIGHTS

The United Nations Convention on the Rights of the Child (CRC) describes three categories of rights that pertain to all children: protection, provision, and participation.

**Protection:** All children have the right to live free of physical and emotional harm. They also have the right to be free from sexual exploitation of any nature and cannot be forced to work under the age of 16.

**Provision:** All children have the right to receive adequate food, shelter, seasonal clothing, as well as proper medical and dental care.

**Participation:** All children have the right to be involved in important decisions about their well-being. Children over the age of 12 must be invited to attend important meetings about them such as a plan of care.

## Rights in Residential Care

1. Reasonable privacy
2. Uncensored mail
3. Receive family visits (visits for CAS wards must be approved by the CAS)
4. Spiritual, religious, and cultural instruction if requested
5. Free of corporal punishment
6. Receive proper education and recreation
7. Not to be detained or locked up and not to be unduly restricted
8. Receive medical and dental care
9. Adequate food and clothing
10. Consulted and heard regarding major decisions
11. Participate in the development of his or her plan of care
12. Able to speak in private with lawyer, CAS worker, advocate, or ombudsman
13. Informed of complaints procedures
14. Informed of their rights

# RESIDENTIAL SERVICES

The roots of Child and Youth Work began in residential services when it was realized that individuals who lived in long-term facilities need competent and trained professionals to care for them.

CYWs are employed to meet the day-to-day needs of the residents. Tasks in a residential program are varied and do not just pertain to counselling, although counselling is a very important feature of the job. Children must be awakened in the morning, assisted with education/employment programs, food must be prepared for meals, medication dispensed, recreational programming, therapeutic programming, medical appointments, supervision of family visits, attend meetings, write reports, manage behaviour, put children to bed, and any other tasks that may arise throughout the day.

Public opinion has always been divided regarding the pros and cons of residential care. Those who feel more negatively find residences restrictive, intrusive, and expensive. At times they also express concern for society's lack of tolerance for certain behaviours that do not fit the "norm" or may be considered deviant. Those who have a more positive opinion feel that residential care offers an increased opportunity to provide intensive treatment interventions for those who need it as it is available 24 hours a day and 7 days a week.

## Licensing

Licensing provisions for children's residences are established by legislation and regulation and are intended to ensure that minimum acceptable standards of care are provided to children and youth in residential care. Ministry licensing inspections include the completion of a licensing checklist covering such things as a review of the premises, the services provided, and the adequacy of the organization's policies and procedures.

The Ministry of Community, Family and Children's Services began licensing residential programs in 1980. Since that time, all agencies that provide residential programming with client numbers ranging from 4 to 120 must be licensed on a yearly basis.

Failure to comply with the CFSA licensing standards set out by the Ministry may result in the residence license being revoked and funding withdrawn.

## Treatment Method

Residential care facilities in North America generally ascribe to six treatment models. Although there are programs that use certain models exclusively, most programs use a blend of several approaches in the development of their treatment philosophy.

1. **Medical Model:** The medical model tends to see a mental health problem as an illness or disease requiring medication and/or psychotherapy. Medication is used to change biochemical processes in the brain that are believed to contribute to the mental health problem. Diagnosis is made from the DSM IV-TR (*Diagnostic and Statistical Manual IV-Text Revision* is a guide for assessing and diagnosing mental disorders). Assessment and treatment is pathology-based.

2. **Social Behavioral Model:** The client must adapt to societal norms. Personal and psychological growth will occur if behaviour is changed.

3. **Psycho-Educational Model:** Every event is a potential learning opportunity and learning is a two-way process between the individual and the world. Cognitive behavioural therapy (CBT) is an example of an evidence-based approach that might be used within the social behavioural model and/or the psycho-educational model. CBT posits a human framework that can be divided into four domains: cognitive (how we think), emotional (how we feel), behaviour (how we act), and physiological (physical well-being). CBT theory maintains that all four domains intersect and interact with one another. When change occurs in one domain this in turn can affect the other domains, i.e., if you can change the way you think then you can change the way you act or behave.

4. **Systems Model:** Family, community, school, etc., are parts that are larger than the whole and we must understand the context in which behaviour occurs. We must understand the parts of the system and how they interact with one another. Accept the fact that behaviour is complex and the child is not the solitary problem. Social workers are generally trained in this perspective. One example is multi-systemic therapy.

5. **Correctional Model:** Must effectively punish antisocial behaviour by restricting personal liberties. This model has changed dramatically over the past decade and will be studied in Unit IV.

6. **Diversionary Model:** Acquisition of new values/skills will divert the person from further problems. Replace anti-social behaviors with pro-social behaviors, i.e., may be through work on a farm, focus on a trade, wilderness camp, or other similar programs.

## TYPES OF RESIDENTIAL PROGRAMS

There are many different types of residential programs available in the province. As much as possible, children are placed in the type of facility that best meets their individual needs. Residential programs are funded according to their specific category.

The types of residential programs are defined below.

1. **Children's Aid Societies:** Any residential services supervised by a Children's Aid Society. These would include foster homes, treatment homes, and assessment homes.

2. **Foster Homes:** Private family homes where residential care is provided for not more than four children (unrelated to the foster parents) under the supervision of the Children's Aid Society.

3. **Secure Detention/Secure Custody:** A place of secure containment or restraint for young persons who meet the criteria for secure detention or custody specified in The Youth Criminal Justice Act.

4. **Open Custody/Open Detention Homes:** Community-based residential facilities for young persons who have been sentenced or are awaiting sentencing under The Youth Criminal Justice Act.

5. **Independent Group Homes:** A transitional care program stressing skills and self-dependence. Any young person can be referred from other services: i.e., CAS, CMHC, and YCJA.

6. **Extended Family Homes:** Homes that are operated by a parent agency to provide care for children in a foster-home-type setting. The capacity for these homes is usually from two to four children.

7. **Children's Mental Health Centres:** Residential treatment and child and family intervention facilities for children with social, emotional, behavioural, and psychiatric problems, formerly listed facilities under the Mental Health Act.

8. **Child and Adolescent Units in Hospitals:** In-patient comprehensive care to children and adolescents up to the age of 18 who are experiencing acute psychiatric symptoms. Unit functions usually include multidisciplinary assessment, initiation of treatment, and discharge planning. Some units also provide after-care services in the areas of case management and day treatment.

9. **Maternity Homes:** Residential care facilities that provide prenatal and postnatal counselling and support for pregnant youths and teen single parents and their children. These programs are often called Pre and Post Natal Residential Services.

10. **Private Operators:** Residential programs that provide support for children and youths with social, emotional, and behavioural problems. These programs are operated by for-profit agencies that usually charge a "per diem" rate per each child/youth living in the facility.

11. **DH Community Accommodation:** A small residential facility for children with developmental handicaps.

12. **DH Community Facilities:** Institutional residential facilities for developmentally handicapped children.

# DUTY TO REPORT

## TORONTO CHILD ABUSE CENTRE
## ONTARIO ASSOCIATION OF CHILDREN'S AID SOCIETIES

The CFSA recognizes that society at large has a responsibility for the welfare of children. Both members of the public and professionals who work with children are legally required to report to a Children's Aid Society **immediately** when child abuse or child protection issues are suspected.

In Ontario, the report can be made to a Catholic Children's Aid Society, Jewish Family and Child Service, a Children's Aid Society, and in most cases Native Child and Family Services.

People working with children are responsible for reporting suspicions of child abuse, **not** for proving whether or not child abuse has occurred. It is the responsibility of a Children's Aid Society to investigate, with police where necessary, and decide on the best plan for the child.

The person who suspects that a child may have been abused or is at risk for abuse must report it immediately to a Children's Aid Society, **and cannot ask anyone else to report for him/ her.** If you work with an agency or program, inform your immediate supervisor of your intention to call a Children's Aid Society. Do not discuss your suspicions with anyone, including your supervisor, until you have consulted with a child protection worker. The supervisor should provide support. However, even if he/she does not want you to make the call, you **must** follow through on your legal responsibility and call a Children's Aid Society.

Respect the confidentiality of everyone involved in a suspicion of child abuse. A Children's Aid Society must also respect confidentiality and details of the case cannot be shared.

If a person has more suspicions or information about a child, then a Children's Aid Society must be contacted again, even if other reports have been made before.

For the purposes of the CFSA, in Ontario a person is a child from birth until his/her 16th birthday.

The CFSA defines the term "child in need of protection" and sets out specifically what must be reported to a Children's Aid Society. It includes neglect, physical, sexual, and emotional abuse, and risk of harm.

It is important to note that a person does not need to be certain that a child is being abused. It is enough to have "reasonable grounds" to suspect abuse is or may be taking place. If a person reports suspected child abuse, he/she cannot be sued if it is proven that the report was made in good faith and not to cause trouble for anyone.

If you are not sure if you should be reporting suspicions of child abuse, call a Children's Aid Society to discuss your concerns with a child protection worker.

Persons who work with children in a professional capacity are recognized as having a special awareness that increases their obligation to report. Failure to report actual or suspected abuse concerning information obtained during professional duties is a criminal offense. A conviction carries a fine of up to $1,000.00. A professional's duty to report supersedes any other obligations regarding client confidentiality.

Persons who are involved with children in a professional capacity include but are not restricted to the following:

- child and youth care counselors
- health care professionals, including physicians, nurses, dentists, pharmacists, and psychologists
- priests, rabbis, and other members of the clergy
- teachers, teacher's assistants and school principals
- operators and employees of day care centres
- social workers and family counsellors
- solicitors
- peace officers and coroners
- youth and recreation workers

There are some relationships that are considered confidential, for example between a doctor and patient, or between clergy and members of the congregation. However, a confidence cannot be kept if child abuse is suspected. No matter what the relationship between people, one must always follow through on **the duty to report** suspicions of child abuse. (The only exception for "privileged" information is in the lawyer-client relationship.)

Although anonymous calls can be made, it is more difficult for authorities to follow-up on the case, gather information and protect the child. It is in the best interests of the child that the reporter leaves his/her identifying information. Remember, the person who reported is protected from having his/her name disclosed.

**Note:** For exact wording from the Act, please see *Duty to Report* legislation excerpted from the Child and Family Services Act that is located in the Appendices of this handbook.

## WHAT IS CHILD ABUSE?

It is important to note that students enrolled in the Child and Youth Care Program at Humber College will be taking several in-depth courses that cover the clinical, ethical, and professional issues related to this topic. The following is meant as a general overview and is to be studied in context of legislation and community resources only.

Generally, child abuse is divided into five categories:

1. Neglect
2. Physical
3. Sexual
4. Emotional
5. Exposure to domestic violence

## NEGLECT

Neglect is when a parent/caregiver does not provide for the basic emotional and physical needs of the child on an ongoing basis. Emotional abuse includes all acts, which result in the absence of a nurturing environment for the child. Children who are neglected physically and emotionally may not develop normally. Some children may suffer permanent damage. Examples of neglect include not providing the proper:

- food
- clothing
- housing
- supervision
- safe surroundings
- personal health care
- medical and mental health care
- education

## PHYSICAL ABUSE

Physical abuse includes anything a parent/caregiver does that results in physical harm to a child. Physical abuse may happen if a child is punished harshly, even though the parent/caregiver may not have meant to hurt the child. Physical abuse may result in a minor injury (such as a bruise) to a more serious injury that could cause lasting damage or death (from shaking a child).

Examples of physical abuse include:

- bruises
- marks in the shape of objects or hand prints
- shaking
- burns
- human bite marks
- fractures of the skull, arms, legs, and ribs
- female genital mutilation

## SEXUAL ABUSE

Sexual abuse occurs when a person uses power over a child, and involves the child in any sexual act. This "abuser" is more powerful due to age, intelligence, physical strength, control over the child, and the child's need to be taken care of by others. The offender may get the child to participate by using threats, bribes, lying, and taking advantage of the child's trust. Most sex offenders are people the children know.

Sexual abuse includes involving the child in acts such as:

• fondling (touching the child in a sexual way)
• getting the child to touch the adult inappropriately
• oral sex
• inserting fingers, penis, or objects into the vagina or anus
• the adult exposes him/herself to the child
• allowing a child to read or watch pornography
• involving a child in pornography or prostitution

## EMOTIONAL ABUSE

Emotional abuse typically has been a difficult form of abuse to define, because it often does not involve a specific incident or visible injury and its effects may not surface until later in a child's development. Children who witness violence in their home may suffer permanent emotional damage.

A parent/caregiver who continually uses any of the following when interacting or disciplining a child is emotionally abusing the child:

• rejecting (I wish you were never born)
• criticizing (Why can't you ever do anything right?)
• insulting (I can't believe you are so stupid)
• humiliating (embarrassing child in front of others)
• isolating (not allowing child to play with friends)
• terrorizing (the police will come and take you away)
• corrupting (swearing in front of child, getting child to participate in breaking the law)
• not responding to a child in an emotional or nurturing way
• punishing a child for exploring the environment

## EXPOSURE TO DOMESTIC VIOLENCE

In this case children are exposed to violence between persons who have intimate relationships. These children display emotional and behavioural problems as though they were physically abused. Exposure to domestic violence is generally considered to be part of emotional abuse.

# GENERAL OVERVIEW OF DISCLOSURES

This segment is included as a matter of interest and as a general instruction in context of the legislative material covered in this course. It is not intended as an in-depth study of clinical or child and youth care practice.

A child who has been a victim of child abuse may, under the proper circumstances, disclose abuse incidents to adults or others that they trust.

If a child comes to you and discloses that he/she has been the victim of abuse, it is not up to you to try to prove your suspicions. Trying to do this may contaminate or ruin the investigation and may put the child at further risk. Leave the investigation to be done by the people who are the experts. There are, however, some general guidelines regarding how to respond in such situations:

**Control your emotions**

- Try to remain calm and relaxed
- Do not looked shocked, disgusted, or say disrespectful things about who you think may have abused the child
- If you feel that you cannot control your feelings, call your supervisor or a trusted colleague or friend to talk

**Offer comfort and support by letting children know that**

- They were very brave to tell
- You are sorry that this has happened to them
- They are not alone – this happens to other children too
- You will do everything you can to help
- You are there to support them

**Do not say things like**

- How can you say such things about…?
- Liar
- That man has ruined you forever
- How could you let him/her do those things to you?
- Why didn't you tell me this before?

## Be aware of the child's ages and skills

- Accept the words that the child uses to describe the incident (including slang words)
- Do not correct or change the words that the child uses
- It is extremely important for the investigation that the child's words are used when telling what happened

## Ask open-ended questions

- Can you tell me more about that?
- How did you get that bruise?
- Can you tell me what happened?

## Do not

- Ask questions of a leading nature or questions that suggest what happened
- Question what the child tells you, i.e., are you sure it was your uncle?
- Add your own words
- Ask children why – this could imply blame
- Try to change the mind of a child who has recanted/changed the story
- Keep asking more questions because you want to try to prove abuse

## Respect the person who discloses

- If a child/adult is telling, listen
- If a child/adult is quiet, do not try to make him/her talk
- Do not ever use force to undress a child to see injuries
- Do not ever show off a child's injuries to others

## Tell the child what will happen next

- Do not make promises that you can't keep, for example, do not agree to keep what the child said a "secret." It is important to explain to the child that some secrets must be shared in order to get help, or to keep people from being hurt.
- Answer the child's questions as simply and honestly as possible. Never make up answers.
- Do not tell the child to keep any of your discussions with him/her a secret.

## Interesting Links

- Metro Toronto CAS: www.casmt.on.ca
- Ontario Association of Children's Aid Societies: www.oacas.org
- Child Welfare League of Canada: www.cwlc.ca
- Toronto Child Abuse Centre: www.tcac.on.ca
- Kids Help Phone: www.kidshelpphone.ca
- Children's Mental Health Ontario: www.cmho.org/
- Voices for Children: www.voices4children.org/
- Ministry of Children and Youth Services: www.children.gov.on.ca
- Justice for Children and Youth: www.jfcy.org/

## The Ontario Human Rights Code

The Ontario Human Rights Code is for everyone. It is a provincial law that gives everybody equal rights and opportunities without discrimination in specific areas such as jobs, housing, and services. The goal of the Code is to prevent discrimination and harassment because of race, colour, age, gender, and handicap, to name some of the sixteen grounds cited. For more information contact www.ohrc.on.ca or 1-800-387-9080 or 416-326-9511.

## The Employment Standards Act (ESA)

The ESA sets out rights of employees and requirements that apply to employers in most Ontario workplaces. It is provincial legislation that has been in force since 2000. For more information please contact www.labour.gov.on.ca or 416-326-7160 or 1-800-531-5551.

## Occupational Health and Safety Act (OHSA)

The OHSA came into force on October 1, 1979. The main purpose of the Act is to protect workers from health and safety hazards on the job. It sets out duties for all workplace parties and rights for workers. It establishes procedures for dealing with workplace hazards and provides for enforcement of the law where compliance has not been achieved voluntarily.

Workers and employers must share the responsibility for occupational health and safety. This concept of an internal responsibility system is based on the principle that the workplace parties themselves are in the best position to identify health and safety problems and to develop solutions. Ideally, the internal responsibility system involves everyone, from the company chief executive officer to the worker. How well the system works depends upon whether there is a complete, unbroken chain of responsibility and accountability for health and safety.

# THE MENTAL HEALTH ACT

There are three main Acts that outline rights with respect to mental health services in Ontario. The Mental Health Act is a set of rules determined by the Ontario legislature that assigns doctors and psychiatric facilities certain powers and gives patients particular rights. These laws apply in child and adolescent hospital psychiatric units and psychiatric hospitals but not mental health clinics. The Health Care Consent Act deals with rules for consenting, or agreeing, to treatment. The Substitute Decisions Act deals with how decisions can be made for a person and the appointment of powers of attorney for personal care and property.

As stated, the Mental Health Act is a piece of provincial legislation. It deals with:

- guidelines for admitting a person to a psychiatric facility as a voluntary or involuntary patient
- the rights of patients in psychiatric facilities
- guidelines for issuing, renewing, or terminating community treatment orders

Brian's Law (formerly known as Bill 68) amended the Mental Health Act and the Health Care Consent Act in 2000. In particular, it introduced community treatment orders and new criteria for involuntary commitment to psychiatric facilities. Before December 1, 2000, the Mental Health Act did not address the issue of community-based treatment. The new law will allow some persons who need treatment for a mental illness to be on a community treatment order, so they can receive treatment outside the hospital. For example, under the old law, a person with a serious mental illness might stay in the hospital, while under the new law, the person can be treated in the community. Community treatment orders can be signed by a physician to compel treatment of a person with a serious mental illness in the community.

# THE HEALTH CARE CONSENT ACT

The Health Care Consent Act deals with guidelines for informed consent for treatment, personal care services, or admission to a long-term care facility and with the roles and responsibilities of substitute decision-makers. The Health Care Consent Act came into force in 1996 (amended 1998, 2000, 2002, 2004, 2006).

Children and youth can consent to health care treatment according to their ability to understand the treatment they are seeking. Consent to treatment in Ontario is not based on chronological age.

- **Consent and Capacity Board**
  The Consent and Capacity Board is an independent body created by the Ontario provincial government. It conducts hearings under the *Mental Health Act*, the *Health Care Consent Act*, the *Substitute Decisions Act*, and the *Personal Health Information Protection Act*.

- **Office of the Public Guardian and Trustee**
  The Office of the Public Guardian and Trustee (OPGT) is responsible for protecting mentally incapable people, among other duties. Resources on the OPGT site include a Guide to the Substitute Decisions Act, a Power of Attorney Kit, information on the role of the OPGT in making substitute health care decisions, information about regulated forms, becoming a guardian, the Capacity Assessment Office, and more.

- **Psychiatric Patient Advocate Office (PPAO)**
  The PPAO is a provincial advocacy program with the mandate to advance the legal and civil rights of psychiatric patients in the province's psychiatric hospitals, and to empower patients to make informed decisions about their lives, care, and treatment. The PPAO provides independent and confidential advocacy services and rights advice to consumers of, and those seeking access to, psychiatric services. Information and patient rights guides are available.

# PRIVACY ISSUES AND PRIVACY LEGISLATION IN ONTARIO

As a CYW you may find yourself employed by youth serving agencies that are governed by this type of legislation. It is always good practice to review the agency's policy and procedures manuals and to ask your supervisor about relevant quality assurance and privacy issues.

Since January 1, 1988, the Information and Privacy Commissioner of Ontario (IPC) has acted independently of government to uphold and promote open government and the protection of personal privacy in Ontario. The Information and Privacy Commissioner is appointed by the Ontario Legislature. This independence from the government of the day allows the Commissioner to be impartial when carrying out duties under the Acts.

The role of the IPC is set out in three statutes: the Freedom of Information and Protection of Privacy Act, the Municipal Freedom of Information and Protection of Privacy Act and the Personal Health Information Protection Act. Under the three Acts, the IPC:

- Resolves access to information appeals and complaints when government or health care practitioners and organizations refuse to grant requests for access or correction;
- Investigates complaints with respect to personal information held by government or health care practitioners and organizations;

- Conducts research into access and privacy issues;
- Comments on proposed government legislation and programs; and
- Educates the public about Ontario's access and privacy laws.

## PERSONAL HEALTH INFORMATION PROTECTION ACT (PHIPA)

The Health Information Protection Act came into force in Ontario in 2004. It is a provincial law that is guaranteed to ensure that personal health information is private, confidential, and secure. The Act consists of two parts: The Personal Health Information Act (PHIPA) and The Quality of Care Information Protection Act (QCIPA).

PHIPA is a new law that will help keep patients' personal health information private, confidential, and secure by imposing rules related to its collection, use, and disclosure. It is the responsibility of the Office of the Information and Privacy Commissioner of Ontario (IPC) to ensure that government organizations abide by PHIPA.

## ONTARIO'S FREEDOM OF INFORMATION AND PROTECTION OF PRIVACY ACT

The purpose of the Act is to provide the public the right of access to government-held information; provide an individual the right of access to his/her own personal information; and impose a duty on government employees to protect individual privacy.

## THE MUNICIPAL FREEDOM OF INFORMATION AND PROTECTION OF PRIVACY ACT

This Act applies to local government organizations, including municipalities; police services boards; school boards; conservation authorities; and boards of health and transit commissions.

The Act requires that local government organizations protect the privacy of an individual's personal information existing in government records. It also gives individuals the right to request access to municipal government information, including most general records and records containing their own personal information.

## THE PRIVACY ACT AND THE PERSONAL INFORMATION AND ELECTRONIC DOCUMENTS ACT

The federal Privacy Act took effect on July 1, 1983. This Act requires approximately 150 federal government departments and agencies to respect privacy rights by limiting the collection, use, and disclosure of personal information. The Privacy Act gives citizens the right to access and ask for correction of personal information about themselves held by these federal government organizations.

Individuals are also protected by the federal Personal Information Protection and Electronic Documents Act (PIPEDA) that sets the ground rules for how private sector organizations may collect, use, or disclose personal information in the course of their business activities. The federal government may excuse organizations or activities in provinces that have their own privacy laws if they are "substantially similar" to the federal law. Supervision of both federal laws rests with the Privacy Commissioner of Canada who is authorized to receive and investigate complaints. For more information contact www.privcom.gc.ca or 1-800-282-1376.

## THE CHILDREN'S LAW REFORM ACT (BILL 22-2010)

The Children's Law Reform Act deals with the custody rights of parents who are separated. Parents can file for custody through the provincial government. The Ontario government has jurisdiction on cases that are filed while a child resides in Ontario. Bill 22 of the Act seeks to make amendments that will emphasize the importance of children's relationships with their parents and grandparents:

Subsection 20 (2.1) of the Act requires parents and others with custody of children to refrain from unreasonably placing obstacles to personal relations between the children and their grandparents.

Subsection 24 (2) of the Act contains a list of matters that a court must consider when determining the best interests of a child. The Bill amends that subsection to include a specific reference to the importance of maintaining emotional ties between children and grandparents and the willingness of each person applying for custody to facilitate as much contact with each parent and grandparent as is consistent with the best interests of the child.

Subsection 24 (2.1) of the Act requires the court to give effect to the principle that a child should have as much contact with each parent and grandparent as is consistent with the best interests of the child.

As of March 1, 2010, there are special requirements for a person seeking custody of a child who is not his or her child. Non-parents must provide a recent police records check (completed within the previous 60 days) and authorize the children's aid societies in areas where they have lived to provide a report that indicates if they have been involved with the person. The court office will also check the court's records and prepare a list of all previous family cases that involve the non-parent or the child. If requested by the judge, they can also prepare a list of all previous criminal court files that involve the non-parents.

# UNIT 3

## YOUTH CRIMINAL JUSTICE ACT (YCJA)

## HISTORY OF YOUTH JUSTICE IN CANADA

### JUVENILE DELINQUENTS ACT (1908–1984)

In 1908 the *Juvenile Delinquents Act* (*JDA*) was proclaimed. It was amended in 1929. This Act recognized that children needed to be treated differently than adults even when they committed a criminal offence. The *JDA* governed children committing offences between the ages of 7 and 18. This Act represented a major philosophical change concerning juvenile delinquent treatment. Before 1908, children in conflict with the law were treated like adult criminals, often receiving harsh sentences for fairly minor crimes. Furthermore, despite provisions in the 1982 Canada Criminal Code, they were frequently detained with adults while awaiting trial and sentenced to adult prisons.

The *JDA* emphasized the aid and protection of juvenile delinquents. This policy emphasized compassion for youth, and the importance of assisting troubled youth through guidance, rather than imprisonment. Under the *JDA*, children in trouble with the law were not charged with breaking a specific statute. Instead, they were charged with "delinquency." Judges had enormous discretion in sentencing juvenile delinquents. A child could be placed in foster care, pay a fine, or be institutionalized until the age of 21.

Challenges to the *JDA*'s welfare approach emerged after World War II as sentiments about youth shifted from children being viewed as objects of state protection to a view of children as "subjects" and "persons with dignity and rights." After the enactment of the Canadian Charter of Rights and Freedoms in 1982, it became increasingly clear that the lack of legal rights for youth within the *JDA* were inconsistent with the protections outlined in the Charter. These challenges led to the creation of the Young Offenders Act in 1984.

# THE YOUNG OFFENDERS ACT (1984–2003)

The Young Offenders Act (*YOA*) governed children committing offences between the ages of 12 and 18. Those children under 12 who were breaking the law were to be dealt with by their parents or the Children's Aid Society. The purpose of the *YOA* was to shift from a social welfare approach to making youth take responsibility for their actions. The lack of clear legislative direction was an important factor contributing to problems in the youth justice system and with the *YOA*:

- The system lacked a clear and coordinated youth justice philosophy
- Canada had the highest youth incarceration rate in the Western world, including the United States
- The courts were over-used for minor cases that could be better dealt with outside the courts
- Sentencing decisions by the courts resulted in unfairness in youth sentencing, i.e., a youth in Barrie, Ontario might receive six months custody for something that would only get probation in Toronto
- The *YOA* did not guarantee effective reintegration of a young person after being released from custody
- The process for transfer to the adult system resulted in unfairness, complexity, and delay
- The system did not make a clear distinction between serious violent offences and less serious offences
- The system did not give sufficient recognition to the concerns and interests of victims

Following many years of public and political criticism, the Young Offenders Act was replaced by the Youth Criminal Justice Act (*YCJA*). On February 4, 2002, Parliament passed Bill C-7, the Youth Criminal Justice Act. The act was proclaimed in force on April 1, 2003.

## YOUTH CRIMINAL JUSTICE ACT (2003–PRESENT)

The *YCJA* builds on strengths of the *YOA* and introduces significant reforms that address weaknesses in the *YOA*.

The new legislation should be seen as part of the federal government's broad approach to youth crime and the reform of Canada's youth justice system.

*The YCJA differs from the YOA in several ways:*

1. It contains a DECLARATION OF PRINCIPLE that removes any uncertainty about how the Act should be interpreted.

2. It expresses the philosophy that the needs of society and the offender are not in conflict.
3. It increases the number of extrajudicial measures available.
4. It reintroduces the concept of Youth Justice Committees, last used under the *JDA*. Made up of groups of citizens, the committees' purpose is to develop community-based solutions to youth offences. These can include extrajudicial measures such as restitution, arranging community support for the youth, or arranging a meeting between the victim and the young offender.
5. It establishes that the court process is reserved for more serious offences. Police must consider all other options (such as a warning or making restitution) before laying charges.
6. It clarifies the conditions for sentencing youth into custody. This takes away some of the subjective power of previous sentencing from youth court judges.
7. It makes provisions for reintegrating youth in custody back into society. The Act introduces a graduated sentence, where youth spend two-thirds of their time in custody, and one-third in the community under supervision.
8. It addresses rights of victims.
9. The *YCJA* places emphasis on the importance of rights for all young people, by specifically referring to the *United Nations Convention on the Rights of the Child* within the Preamble.

**For more information visit:**

http://www.justice.gc.ca/eng/pi/yj-jj/ycja-lsjpa/back-hist.html

# THE YOUTH CRIMINAL JUSTICE ACT

The *Youth Criminal Justice Act* contains both a Preamble and a Declaration of Principle to clarify the principles and objectives of the youth justice system.

## The Preamble

- Society has a responsibility to address the developmental challenges and needs of young persons.
- Communities and families should work in partnership.
- Accurate information about youth crime should be publicly available.
- Young persons have rights and freedoms.
- The youth justice system should take account of interests of victims.

The **Declaration of Principle** sets out the policy framework for the interpretation of the legislation. This Declaration provides that:

- The objectives of the youth justice system are to prevent crime; rehabilitate and reintegrate young persons into society; and ensure meaningful consequences for offences.
- The youth justice system must reflect the fact that young persons lack the maturity of adults.
- Young persons are to be held accountable through interventions that are fair and in proportion to the seriousness of the offence.
- Interventions should reinforce respect for societal values, encourage the repair of harm done, be meaningful to the young person, respect gender, ethnic, cultural, and linguistic differences and respond to the needs of Aboriginal young persons and of young persons with special requirements.
- Youth justice proceedings require special guarantees to protect the rights of young people; courtesy, compassion, and respect for victims.

In addition, the *YCJA* includes other more specific principles to guide decisions at key points in the youth justice process: Extrajudicial Measures, Youth Sentencing, and Custody and Supervision.

Note: For exact wording of The Declaration of Principle excerpted from the *YCJA* please go to the Appendices section at the end of the handbook.

## RISK FACTORS, PROTECTIVE FACTORS, AND YOUTH OFFENDING

The Federal government looked at research related to specific factors when developing sentencing options and programming guidelines for the *YCJA*.

In order to understand the basic principles of the *YCJA* we need to understand what is meant by risk and protective factors.

The "ecological model" recognizes that each person functions within a complex network of individual, family, community, school, and environmental worlds that impact (or change) their (ability or) capacity to avoid risk.

**Risk Factors** are defined as scientifically established factors or determinants for which there is strong objective evidence of a causal relationship to a problem. For example, exposure to domestic violence at an early age can increase risk of sexually offending behavior in adolescents.

**Protective Factors** are features that can potentially decrease the likelihood of engaging in a risk behavior or positive dynamic indicators that can decrease a negative outcome. Call protective factors "assets" if you like. These factors can influence the level of risk an individual experiences and can also change the relationship between the risk and outcome or behavior. These factors can lower risk factors or "improve the odds."

*Research on risk and protective factors related to youth crime has identified the following kinds of risk factors:*

## Youth Crime Risk Factors

| Individual risk factors | Characteristics such as gender, age, and physiological, biological, and psychological characteristics. Risk factors include hyperactivity, limited attention span, restlessness, risk taking, poor social skills, and certain beliefs and attitudes. In addition, adolescents with certain disabilities (for example, emotional disturbances, attention deficit disorder, and specific learning disabilities) are more likely to display antisocial behaviour. |
|---|---|
| Family factors | Involves the support the family offers a child. Risk factors that predict early onset and chronic patterns of antisocial behaviour include harsh and ineffective parental discipline, lack of parental involvement, family conflict, parental criminality, child abuse and neglect, and witnessing domestic violence. |
| School factors | Involve peer interactions, how schools respond to certain kinds of behaviour, academic achievement, and so forth. Risk factors include low school involvement, academic and social failure, lack of clarity and follow-through in rules and policies, poor and/or inconsistent administrative support, and few allowances for individual differences. Inconsistent and inequitable disciplinary practices also contribute to risk. |
| Peer factors | Overlaps with school factors, but also involves who a young person "hangs with" outside school, particularly when that young person no longer attends school regularly. Risk factors include having peers who are pro-crime, peer rejection, and discrimination. |
| Community factors | Includes physical environment, economic and recreational opportunities, existing social support, and other issues that impact the functioning of residents. Some communities lack features that help prevent antisocial lifestyles such as before and after school programming, recreational opportunities, and prosocial adult mentors. When emotionally or financially supporting friends and employment are missing, youth may try to get friends and money through antisocial behaviour. |
| Environmental factors | Involve larger social issues such as social values, prevailing ideology, poverty, racial/ethnic discrimination, social policy, and impact of the media. For instance, environmental factors play an important role in contributing to a culture of violence among a particular group of people in a given community (poverty and general disenfranchisement of young people in our society are possible examples). |

*Research on risk and protective factors related to youth crime has identified the following kinds of protective factors:*

## Youth Crime Protective Factors

| | |
|---|---|
| **Social Bonding** | Strengthening children's bonds with family members, friends, teachers, and other socially responsible adults. |
| **Healthy Standards** | Having parents, teachers, community leaders and others who lead by example, holding clearly stated expectations for children's behavior. |
| **Opportunities for Involvement** | Affording children opportunities to feel involved and valued in their families, schools, and communities. |
| **Social & Learning Skills** | Equipping children with the social, reasoning and practical skills they need to take full advantage of opportunities. |
| **Recognition and Praise** | Ensuring that childrens' contributions and positive behavior are recognized, thus giving them an incentive to continue. |

As a point of interest, the latest research shows that children who feel a bond, or an attachment, to their schools are less likely to develop problems in adolescence. Not surprisingly, students who are not committed to school are at an increased risk.

## FEATURES OF THE YCJA

### *Extrajudicial Measures*

These are measures that do not involve the courts.

Police and prosecutors are specifically authorized to use various types of extrajudicial measures:

- *Taking no further action*
- *Warnings* are informal warnings by police officers
- *Police cautions* are more formal warnings by the police
- *Crown cautions* are similar to police cautions but prosecutors give the caution after the police refer the case to them
- *Referrals* are referrals of young persons by police officers to community programs or agencies that may help them and therefore prevent further conflict with the law

## *Extrajudicial Sanctions*

Extrajudicial sanctions, known as alternative measures under the *YOA*, are a type of extrajudicial measure that is intended for more serious offences and offenders than would be dealt with by warnings, cautions, and referrals. In comparison to other types of extrajudicial measures, a more formal set of rules applies to extrajudicial sanctions.

Extrajudicial sanctions may only be used if:
- Other extrajudicial measures would not be adequate
- It is part of an existing program in the region
- The person considering using the sanction believes it would be appropriate given the needs of the young person and the needs of society
- The young person has been informed about the sanction, been advised of his/her right to counsel, been given the opportunity to consult counsel and consented to its use
- The young person must have accepted responsibility for the act or omission that forms the basis of the offence. A sanction **cannot** be used if the young person denies the offence or wishes the charge to be dealt with by the court
- The Crown must believe there is sufficient evidence to proceed with a charge

## *Conferences*

The *YCJA* authorizes and encourages the convening of conferences to assist decision-makers in the youth justice system. A *conference* is defined as a group of people brought together to give advice to a police officer, judge, justice of the peace, prosecutor, provincial director, or youth worker who is required to make a decision under the Act. A conference can give advice on decisions such as:

- appropriate judicial measures;
- conditions for release from pre-trial detention;
- appropriate sentences; and,
- plans for reintegrating the young person back into his or her community after being in custody.

A conference could be composed of a variety of people depending on the situation. It could include parents of the young person, the victim and his/her family, police, others who are familiar with the young person and his or her neighbourhood, community agencies, or professionals with a particular expertise needed for a decision. It could also be a professional case conference in which professionals discuss how the young person's needs may best be met and how services in the community can be coordinated to assist the young person.

## *Pre-Trial Detention*

Pre-trial detention is not to be used as a substitute for child protection, mental health, or other social measures.

## *Youth Sentences*

Specific sentencing principles emphasize that the sentence must:

- not be more severe than what an adult would receive for the same offence;
- be similar to youth sentences in similar cases;
- be proportionate to the seriousness of the offence and the degree of responsibility of the young person;
- within the limits of proportionality;
  - be the least restrictive alternative;
  - be the sentencing option that is most likely to rehabilitate and reintegrate the young person; and,
  - promote in the young person a sense of responsibility and an acknowledgement of the harm done by the offence.

## *Sentencing Options*

- *Reprimand.* A reprimand is expected to be essentially a stern lecture or warning from the judge.
- *Intensive support and supervision order.* This sentencing option provides closer monitoring and more concentrated support than a probation officer.
- *Attendance Order* requires the young person to attend a program at specified times and on conditions set by the judge.
- *Deferred custody and supervision order* allows a young person who would otherwise be sentenced to custody to serve the sentence in the community under specific conditions.
- *Intensive rehabilitative custody and supervision order* is a special sentence for serious violent offenders. The Court can make this order if:
  - the young person has been found guilty of a presumptive offence, i.e., murder, attempted murder, manslaughter, aggravated sexual assault, or has a pattern of repeated, serious violent offences;
  - the young person is suffering from a mental or psychological disorder or an emotional disturbance;
  - an individualized treatment plan has been developed;
  - an appropriate program is available and the young person is suitable for admission and consents to admission.

Additional sentencing orders from the *YOA* remain in effect under the *YCJA*. They include:

- fines
- community service orders – require a young person to volunteer a specified number of hours performing volunteer work in the community
- restitution – requires a young person to pay their victim the replacement value of their loss
- reparation – requires a young person to repair or replace damaged/stolen property
- open/secure custody – requires a young person to be detained for a determinant period of time

## The Four "Rs" of the YCJA

- Rehabilitation
- Reintegration
- Rights of young persons as a unique and separate population from that of the adult population (enhanced rights for youth with special needs; enhanced sensitivity to needs of Aboriginal or First Nations young persons)
- Restorative Justice (repairs the harm to the victim and community, makes restitution)

## Adult Sentences

The *YCJA* contains some important changes regarding adult sentencing:

- A pattern of repeated, serious violent offences is added to the list of offences that give rise to the presumption of an adult sentence.
- The age at which the presumption of an adult sentence applies is lowered to 14.
- If the Crown notifies the youth court that it will not be seeking an adult sentence for a presumptive offence, the court may not impose an adult sentence.
- If a youth sentence would be of sufficient length to hold the young person accountable, the court must impose a youth sentence.
- A young person under age 18 who receives an adult sentence is to be placed in a youth facility unless it would not be in the best interests of the young person or would jeopardize the safety of others.

In a Supreme Court of Canada ruling made on May 16, 2008, it was decided that although it was previously the responsibility of young offenders to prove why they should not be punished as adults for serious crimes, the court ruled that placing this onus on youth is unconstitutional. As a result, now the Crown must prove that a youth convicted of a serious violent offence ought to be sentenced as an adult.

## Custody and Supervision in the Community

Under the *YCJA*, every period of custody is to be followed by a period of supervision in the community, as part of the sentence. One-third of the custody sentence must be served in the community, i.e., a 6-month open custody sentence would always be followed by a 3-month community supervision order. The judge, at the time of imposing one of these custody sentences, must clearly state in open court the portion of the sentence to be served in custody and the portion to be served in the community. This must be clearly documented on the young person's Warrant of Committal to Custody.

The *YCJA* contains a list of mandatory conditions that apply to all young persons while under supervision in the community. Additional conditions can be imposed to support the young person. If a young person breaches a condition while in the community, reviews will be held that can result in a change in conditions or a return to custody.

## Reintegration Plans and Reintegration Leaves

When a young person is sentenced to custody, the *YCJA* requires that a youth worker collaborate with the young person to plan for his or her reintegration into the community. The reintegration plan sets out the most effective programs for the young person in order to maximize his or her chances for successful reintegration into the community. While a young person is in custody he/she may not leave the facility without a reintegration leave pass that has been authorized by the provincial director and that specifies the conditions of the pass, i.e., escort status, destination, time and date, purpose of pass, and so on.

## Level of Detention Review

The *YCJA* allows provinces to choose whether decisions about the level of custody are made by either a youth court justice or Provincial Director. Section 85 (5) of the *YCJA* sets out the factors that a Provincial Director must take into account when making a determination about the appropriate level of custody:

    a)   that the appropriate level of custody is the one that is the least restrictive, having regard to:
        (1) the seriousness of the offence in respect of which the young person was committed to custody and the circumstances in which the offence was committed,
        (2) the needs and circumstances of the young person, including proximity to family, school, employment, and support services,
        (3) the safety of other young persons in custody, and
        (4) the interests of society;

(b) that the level of custody should allow for the best possible match of programs to the young person's needs and behaviour, having regard to the findings of any assessment in respect of the young person; and

(c) the likelihood of escape.

The *YCJA* also articulates a general standard of care for youth in the custody and supervision system as one that provides for, "the safe, fair and humane custody and supervision of young persons."

Reviews of a young person's custody placement should occur on an on-going basis rather than only upon admission to custody. Case management planning in secure custody facilities should include the goal of assisting a young person to make a successful argument for placement in an open custody setting at annual or optional review.

## *Custody Review Board (CRB)*

The CRB is a tribunal that conducts reviews and hearings on various matters affecting young persons placed in youth custody facilities or adult maximum security facilities. The CRB is governed by the *Child and Family Services Act* and the *Ministry of Correctional Services Act.*

Section 97 of the *Child and Family Services Act* grants the Board authority to conduct reviews requested by youth who are 12 years of age or older and who have committed an offence between the ages of 12 and 16.

The following decisions are reviewed by the CRB:

• A particular placement where a young person is being held or to which the young person has been transferred;

• A Provincial Director's refusal to authorize the young person's temporary release or reintegration leave;

• A young person's transfer from a place of open custody to a place of secure custody.

Section 52(1) of the Ministry of *Correctional Services Act* grants the Board the authority to conduct reviews requested by individuals who are 16 years of age or older and who have committed an offence between the ages of 16 and 18.

The following decisions are reviewed by the CRB:

• A Provincial Director's decision to hold a young person in or transfer the young person to a maximum security facility;

- A decision about a particular placement where a young person is being held, or to which the young person has been transferred;
- A Provincial Director's refusal to authorize a young person's temporary release or reintegration leave.

## Prison and Reformatories Act

An Act respecting public and reformatory prisons, it sets out guidelines for issues such as: committal, reception and transfer of prisoners and earned remission. If a young person serves a youth sentence in an adult correctional facility (as outlined in sections 89, 92, or 93 of the YCJA), they must be subject to the Prisons and Reformatories Act (PRA) or any other statute, regulation or rule applicable in respect of prisoners or offenders except the records, publication, and information restrictions of the YCJA.

## Publication

A cornerstone of youth justice in Canada is that, as a general rule, the identity of the young person should be protected. However, there are certain exceptions. Under the YCJA, identifying information cannot be published until a youth court has found the young person guilty of the offence and imposed an adult sentence. The YCJA also allows publication of identifying information where a youth sentence is imposed for a presumptive offence. However, there are limitations:

- The court may decide that publication is not appropriate, taking into account the importance of the young person's rehabilitation and public interest
- Publication is not permitted if the prosecutor has notified the court that an adult sentence will not be sought for the presumptive offence

## Bill C-4

Also known as Sébastien's Law [Protecting the Public from Violent Young Offenders]. This name was chosen in memory of Sébastien Lacasse, who, in 2004, was chased down by a group of youths and killed on a Laval, Quebec, street by a 17-year-old.

This Bill was tabled in the House of Commons by the Minister of Justice and Attorney General of Canada, the Honourable Robert Nicholson, and passed on first reading on March 16, 2010. (Note: This bill died on the order table when the election was called on March 26, 2011. It is expected to be reintroduced early in this new session of Parliament along with other law-and-order measures.)

The purpose of the bill is to amend certain provisions of the *YCJA* to emphasize the importance of protecting society and to facilitate the detention of young persons who reoffend or who pose a threat to public safety. More particularly, the bill:

- establishes deterrence and denunciation as sentencing principles similar to the principles provided in the ***adult*** criminal justice system (clause 7);
- expands the case law definition of a violent offence to include reckless behaviour endangering public safety (clause 2);
- amends the rules for pre-sentence detention (also called "pre-trial detention") to facilitate the detention of young persons accused of crimes against property punishable by a maximum term of five years or more (clause 4);
- authorizes the court to impose a prison sentence on a young person who has previously been subject to a number of extrajudicial sanctions (clause 8);
- requires the Crown to consider the possibility of seeking an adult sentence for young offenders 14 to 17 years of age convicted of murder, attempted murder, manslaughter, or aggravated sexual assault (clauses 11 and 18);
- facilitates publication of young offenders' names convicted of violent offences (clauses 20 and 24);
- requires police to keep a record of any extrajudicial measures imposed on young persons so that their criminal tendencies can be documented (clause 25);
- prohibits the imprisonment of young persons in adult correctional facilities (clause 21).

## Some Concerns Regarding Bill C-4

- Changing the primary goal to protection of the public changes the original intention that was to prevent crime, rehabilitate, and reintegrate young persons and ensure meaningful consequences. It ignores Article 3 of the UNCRC where the "best interests of children must be the primary concern in making decisions that may affect them."
- Research demonstrates that deterrence and denunciation are ineffective for adults and even more ineffective for youth. Increasing penalties or increasing rates of incarceration are not associated with reductions in crime rates, nor are lengthier custodial penalties associated with reductions in recidivism rates among individual offenders.
- Proposed amendments would represent a major overhaul of the *YCJA*. These changes would have very serious consequences, resulting in more youths going to jail, for extended periods of time.
- The publication ban could be lifted at any time for the protection of the public. This undermines the young person's ability for rehabilitation and reintegration and violates a child's right to privacy in all stages of the proceedings as declared in Article 16 and 40 of the UNCRC.

In June 2010, the Canadian Bar Association wrote a report on Bill C-4. They noted that although Bill C-4 contains several needed amendments, the proposed legislation as a whole, would mark a significant step backward from the progress that came with the passage of the *YCJA*. For example, the report states that since the implementation of the *YCJA* in 2003, *rates of youth crime have gone consistently down* while incarceration rates of young persons (after sentence) have also gone down. In other words, the *YCJA* is working as intended. Therefore, a question arises of why successful legislation must be amended.

**To read this report**: http://www.cba.org/CBA/submissions/pdf/10-41-eng.pdf

## The Role of Victims under the YCJA

The principles of the *YCJA* specifically recognize concerns of victims. Victims are given information about the proceedings and given an opportunity to participate and be heard.

### *Restorative Justice*

Restorative justice is one way to respond to a criminal act. Restorative justice puts emphasis on the wrong done to a person as well as on the wrong done to the community. It recognizes that crime is both a violation of relationships between specific people and an offence against everyone, i.e., the state or community.

Restorative justice programs involve voluntary participation of the victim of the crime and the offender and ideally members of the community, in discussions. The goal is to "restore" the relationship, fix the damage that has been done, and prevent further crimes from occurring.

Restorative justice requires young persons to recognize the harm they have caused, to accept responsibility for their actions and to be actively involved in improving the situation. Young persons must make reparation to victims, themselves, and the community.

All restorative justice programs have some common elements. They seek healing, forgiveness, and active community involvement. The programs can take place at different times after a crime has occurred—sometimes after charges have been laid; sometimes after an accused has been found guilty of an offence. Some examples of restorative justice programs include:

* victim offender mediation;
* family group conferencing;
* sentencing circles;
* consensus-based decision-making on the sentence; and
* victim offender reconciliation panels.

Good restorative justice programs have well-trained facilitators who are sensitive to the needs of victims and offenders, who know the community in which the crime took place and who understand the dynamics of the criminal justice system.

**For more information visit:** http://www.justice.gc.ca/eng/pi/pcvi-cpcv/res-rep.html

## *Provincial Offences Act*

Governs how charges are processed and prosecuted in the Ontario courts. The Provincial Offences Act applies to all Ontario statutes (and regulations), municipal by-laws, and some federal contraventions.

The Provincial Offences Act contains a section dealing with youth. For example, youth 16 and over are considered an adult, and their parents will not be notified of any charges.

## CANADIAN CRIMINAL CODE AND PROTECTION FOR CHILDREN AND YOUTH

### *Sexual Consent*

In 2008, changes to the Criminal Code of Canada increased the age of consent for nonexploitive sexual activity to 16 years from 14. The age of consent for exploitive activity (prostitution, pornography, or relationship of trust, authority, or dependency) is 18 years.

Youth of 14 or 15 can consent to sexual activity with a person no more than five years older. For example, a youth of 14 years of age may consent to having sexual activity with a 19-year-old, but are deemed incapable of consenting to the same activity with a 20-year-old.

Youth of 12 or 13 may engage in consensual sexual activity with a peer who is no more than two years older. For instance, a 13-year-old may consent to sexual activity with a 15-year-old; however, they are deemed incapable of consenting to sexual activity with a 16-year-old.

Children younger than 12 are still judged incapable of consenting to any sexual activity with any person, regardless of the person's age.

*All sexual activity without valid consent constitutes a sexual assault, regardless of age.*

### *Section 43*

On January 30, 2004, the Supreme Court of Canada released its decision in the case of *Canadian Foundation for Children, Youth and the Law* v. *The Attorney General in Right of Canada*, which concerns the use of force by parents and teachers to correct a child.

The issue was whether Section 43 of the *Criminal Code of Canada* is unconstitutional. Section 43 states that a parent, teacher, or person acting in the place of a parent is justified in using force to correct a child that is under his or her care provided that the force used is reasonable in all of the circumstances.

The Supreme Court of Canada decided that Section 43 of the Criminal Code is constitutional; it found that Section 43 does not violate a child's rights to security of the person and equality, and is not cruel and unusual punishment. The Supreme Court held that Section 43 ensures that the criminal law applies to any use of force that harms a child, but does **not** apply where the use of force "is part of a genuine effort to educate the child, poses no reasonable risk of harm that is more than transitory and trifling, and is reasonable under the circumstances."

The Canadian Foundation for Children, Youth and the Law, argued that Section 43 violates children's *Charter* rights to security of the person, equality and that Section 43 constituted cruel and unusual punishment. The Attorney General of Canada argued that Section 43 reflects a fair balance between interests of children, parents, and Canadian society. Although the federal government does not condone the physical discipline of children, neither does it support the criminalization of parents for disciplinary conduct undertaken in a reasonable way and takes into account the needs and best interests of children.

**For more information refer to:**
http://www.justice.gc.ca/eng/news-nouv/fs-fi/2004/doc_31114.html

## YOUTH JUSTICE LINKS AND REFERENCES

Bala, N., Carrington, P.J. & Roberts, J. (2009). Evaluating the youth criminal justice act after five years: A qualified success. *Canadian Journal of Criminology and Criminal Justice, 51*(2), 131–167.

The Canadian Bar Association. (2010). *Bill C-4 Youth Criminal Justice Act Amendments*. http://www.cba.org/CBA/submissions/pdf/10-41-eng.pdf

Denov, M. S. (2004). Children's rights or rhetoric? Assessing Canada's *Youth Criminal Justice Act* and its compliance with the UN Convention on the Rights of the Child. *International Journal of Children's Rights, 12*(1), 1–20.

Department of Justice Canada. (2004). *Fact Sheet: Section 43 of the Criminal Code (Corporal Punishment)*. http://www.justice.gc.ca/eng/news-nouv/fs-fi/2004/doc_31114.html

Department of Justice Canada. (2010). *Restorative Justice.* http://www.justice.gc.ca/eng/pi/pcvi-cpcv/res-rep.html

Department of Justice Canada. (2002). *Youth Criminal Justice Act*. http://laws-lois.justice.gc.ca/eng/acts/Y-1.5/index.html

Department of Justice Canada. *The Youth Criminal Justice Act: Summary and Background*. http://www.justice.gc.ca/eng/pi/yj-jj/ycja-lsjpa/back-hist.html

Eisler, L. & Schissel, B. (2008). Globalization, justice and the demonization of youth. *International Journal of Social Inquiry, 1*(1), 167–187.

# UNIT 4

## THE EDUCATION ACT

# FACTORS THAT INFLUENCE THE EDUCATIONAL SYSTEM

The Constitution Act gives exclusive authority to each province in Canada to make laws in relation to education. In Ontario, the Ministry of Education and the Ministry of Training, Colleges and Universities are responsible for education. The federal government has constitutional responsibility for education in the Territories.

In 1968 the Ontario Ministry of Education commissioned the Hall Dennis Report. This report indicated there should be no distinction from one type of student to another. It also stated individual progress should occur along a continuum with the choices of experiences and rate of progress dependent upon the student's needs, interests, and own rate of maturing.

In 1970, The Commission on Emotional and Learning Disorders in Children (The C.E.L.D.I.C. Report) focused attention on the urgency to develop approaches to meet special needs. The report also expresses distress at the relative segregation of the school from other sources of help.

The Education Act was proclaimed in 1975 and revised in 1980.

**Note:** Ontario Ministry of Education Website: http://www.edu.gov.on.ca/

## CANADIAN CHARTER OF RIGHTS AND FREEDOMS

Because of the strong "equality rights" language in the Canadian Charter of Rights and Freedoms, the Charter threatened provisions for education that have been in the Constitution since confederation. Therefore a special clause was put into the Charter to prevent this from happening.

The clause guarantees privileges to special schools that operate under denominational or separate provisions, i.e., Roman Catholic or Separate Schools.

This clause especially gives provinces the right to keep anything that existed in the way of schools when that province entered confederation, i.e., "grandfathered."

## AMENDMENTS

There are also two types of procedures that can be followed if amendments/changes or additions need to be made to those parts of the Constitution relating to the assignment of education.

One set of procedures is used when the change affects only one province and a different set of procedures is used if the amendment affects all provinces.

## BILL 82

There have been several large scale amendments to The Education Act since 1980. In 1984 the government enacted Bill 82.

This bill is still in effect today and has profound impact on the education of children in our province. The bill makes the provision of services for exceptional children mandatory for all Boards of Education. This is the legislation that deals with special education services to children and youth in our province.

An exceptional student is defined as a "pupil whose behavioural, communicational, intellectual, physical or multiple exceptionalities are such that he/she is considered to need placement in a special education program." Sec 1 (1) (21)

The fundamental principles in Bill 82 are:

1. the right of every individual to have equal access to the learning experience best suited to his/her needs and
2. the responsibility of every school authority to provide a child-centered learning continuum that invites learning by individual discovery and inquiry.

## THE SAFE SCHOOLS ACT

*The Safe Schools Act* became a part of the *Education Act* in 2000. This is an Ontario bill that was implemented to provide a definitive set of regulations for behavioural infractions that must be issued for students as well as a *Code of Conduct and Police-School Board protocol*. The bill was often referred to as a *zero-tolerance* policy, however, "the presence of mitigating factors in the Act and school board policies precluded it from being strictly defined as a zero tolerance regime". Nonetheless, the bill has been criticized for not providing enough flexibility to schools for disciplining students on a case-by-case basis, preferring instead mandatory suspensions for a wide range of behaviour including verbal abuse and physical violence.

A report commissioned by the *Ontario Human Rights Commission* concluded that "there is a strong perception supported by some empirical evidence that the Act and school board policies are having a disproportionate impact on racial minority students, and students with disabilities."

The McGuinty government conducted a comprehensive review of *The Safe Schools Act* in 2004. Implementation of the Act was found to be inconsistent and unfair. The "one size fits all" approach did not take into account the diverse and complex needs of Ontario students.

On February 1, 2008, Bill 212 *Education Amendment Act (Progressive Discipline and School Safety)* was put into effect to amend the safe schools Act. On February 1, 2010, the latest government safe school initiative, Bill 157 (Keeping our Kids Safe at School) became law.

## PROGRESSIVE DISCIPLINE

Ontario's new approach to making schools safer involves progressive discipline. It is a whole-school approach that utilizes a continuum of prevention programs, interventions, supports, and consequences to address inappropriate student behaviour.

Progressive discipline relies on strategies that promote and foster positive behaviors. Disciplinary measures should be applied within a framework that is not solely punitive, but to one that is both corrective and supportive. Schools should implement a variety of interventions, supports, and consequences that are developmentally appropriate and include learning opportunities for reinforcing positive behaviour while helping students to make good choices.

Progressive discipline enables the principal to choose consequences appropriate to the student's needs and behaviour.

**For more information on suspensions, expulsions and progressive discipline, visit:**

http://www.edu.gov.on.ca/eng/safeschools/NeedtoKnowSExp.pdf

## BILL 157 NEWS – KEEPING OUR KIDS SAFE AT SCHOOL

New legislation, Bill 157 (Keeping our Kids Safe at School) came into effect on February 1st, 2010.

The purpose of this new legislation is to make schools safer by:

1. requiring all school staff to report to principals when they become aware that students may have engaged in incidents for which they could be suspended or expelled;

2. requiring the principal to inform parents of students harmed as a result of an incident for which a student could be suspended or expelled; and

3. requiring that school staff respond if they observe student behaviour likely to have a negative impact on the school climate. This response is to be carried out in accordance with Ministry and school board policy.

**For more information on Bill 157:**
http://www.edu.gov.on.ca/eng/safeschools/KeepKidSafeSchool.pdf

## SPECIAL FEATURES

### Age Requirements

A student is expected to remain in school until the end of the school year he/she turns 18. If a student is receiving a proper education at home or elsewhere, or if he/she cannot attend school due to illness, there may be provisions for formal excuses from the public education system.

An early school leave may be granted to a student as young as 14 years of age. The Board of Education and parents must agree that it is in the best interests of the student to be involved in a different type of productive activity, such as a job-training program. Such "leaves" are extremely rare.

### Ontario School Records

The school maintains a file on each student called an Ontario Student Record (O.S.R.). This file contains copies of all report cards and any other significant information and follows the student no matter where they are educated in Ontario. The student and his/her parents have the right to view the O.S.R. at any time. The principal and teacher also have access to the file. A student over the age of 16 has the right to see the file without the assistance of his/her parents. At this age, parents are not able to view the contents of the O.S.R. without the consent of the student. Parts of the O.S.R. are maintained for 55 years after a student has completed school. This policy is currently under revision.

### Corporal Punishment

Corporal punishment is the deliberate infliction of pain intended as correction or punishment ("corporal" means of, relating to, or affecting the body).

As far back as 1968 the Hall Dennis Report recommended ending the legal approval of corporal punishment in schools. Since 1968 an increasing awareness of its potential for harm has led some provinces to amend their Education Acts to expressly prohibit this method of discipline.

Ontario has not amended the Education to fully prohibit enforcement of Section 43 of the Criminal Code of Canada, which states:

**(Correction of Child by Force)**

Every school teacher, parent or person standing in the place of a parent is justified in using force by way of correction toward a pupil or child, as the case may be, who is under his care, if the force does not exceed what is reasonable under the circumstances. R.S.C., 1985, c.C-4

On Friday, January 30, 2004, the Supreme Court of Canada upheld the so-called "spanking law" but set legal guidelines aimed at ensuring "reasonable" limits:

- Parents will not face criminal charges for "minor" corporal punishment of children aged 2-12.
- Corporal punishment is unacceptable for children under 2 and for teenagers.
- No use of implements other than the open hand, such as rulers or belts.
- No striking of the child on the face or the head.
- Discipline must be for "educational" or "corrective" purposes, not motivated by anger or frustration.
- There must be no lasting bodily harm.
- Punishment must not be "inhuman" or "degrading."
- Corporal punishment in schools is unacceptable. Teachers may restrain students, for example, to escort them from the classroom, but must not hit them.

**For more detailed information regarding this legislation please access the following website**: http://www.cleonet.ca/instance.php?instance_id=2458

## *Section 23 Classrooms*

A Section 23 classroom (the "section" number varies in accordance with legislative changes and this type of class has been referred to as Section 27 and Section 23 in previous years) is the result of an agreement between the Board of Education and the Ministry of Children and Youth Services to meet the academic and behavioural needs of emotionally disturbed children. These classrooms generally have a maximum of 10 students per teacher and CYW. They are generally operated in collaboration with a social service agency.

These educational programs are also referred to as ISA (Intensive Support) Level 4 and are provided by district school boards for school-aged young people, who for various reasons are unable to attend regular schools. "ISA" refers to Intensive Support Amount and relates to funding.

Ministries of Education, Health and Children and Youth Services provide a multi-disciplinary approach. These types of classrooms are referred to as *Section 20 or 23* classes in the education system and as *day treatment* classes in the mental health system but essentially they are one and the same.

Staff working in such program include CYWs, teachers, social workers, art therapists, psychologists, psychiatrists, physiotherapists, and occupational therapists. The term "multi-disciplinary" represents various disciplines working with students (not to the type of discipline meted out to students).

For an overview of Section 23 classrooms, visit http://www.tcdsb.org/section20/Overview.htm

## WHAT IS SPECIAL EDUCATION?

A special education or special ed. program is defined as "an educational program that is based on and modified by the results of a continuous assessment and evaluation of the pupil."

A special education program must include a plan (called I.E.P. or Individual Education Plan) outlining specific objectives and educational services that meet the needs of the pupil or exceptional student. An exceptional student is defined as a "pupil whose behavioral, communicational, intellectual, physical or multiple exceptionalities are such that he/she is considered to need placement in a special education program."

### *Exceptional Students Identification Placement and Review Committee*

When a student has been identified by the teacher and principal as having exceptional learning circumstances, a psychological assessment will be conducted by the Board and an application will be made for an Identification, Placement, and Review Committee (I.P.R.C.) meeting to take place at the Board. This is the only pathway for a student to access special education in Ontario at this time. This meeting involves the participation of appropriate school personnel, parents and the child as well as significant collateral contacts (i.e., CYW, social worker). This meeting determines which category of exceptionality the child fits into and how best to meet the needs of the child. Without this identification process, the school will be unable to provide the support required. Parents must be in agreement with the plan before it can be finalized.

### *Individual Education Plan*

After a completion of an I.P.R.C. meeting, the child's teacher will develop an Individual Education Plan (I.E.P.) to support the student in successfully achieving their goals. There is provision in the Act for an I.E.P. to be developed prior to an I.P.R.C. meeting since it often takes quite a while to schedule the meeting.

## *Individualized Teaching Strategies*

Some examples of individualized teaching strategies that may be identified in an I.E.P. include the following:

- Using special resources such as reading material consistent with the student's reading levels and learning styles
- Videotapes, audiotapes, and other audio visual materials that give learning experiences greater breadth and depth
- Using learning resources that provide direct experiences of seeing and touching (tactile materials)
- Providing enrichments units, additional readings, and other opportunities (i.e., problems to solve) that extend learning
- Simplifying the language of instruction
- Providing opportunities for performance in areas of special talent
- Mentorship programs
- Providing all students with strategies for understanding and accepting exceptional students and integrating them into the regular classroom

## *Individualized Accommodations*

- Extra time to complete classroom assignments
- Allow students to complete tasks or present information in alternate ways, i.e., drama, taped answers, demonstrations, role play, etc.
- Provide for use of scribes
- Use pictorial schedules to assist students in making transitions

## *Special Education Advisory Committees*

Special Education Advisory Committees operate within each board to provide leadership regarding educational needs of exceptional students within the jurisdiction of the board. The committee is composed of members of the Board of Education as well as representatives from other areas who have an interest and investment in educational programming.

## *Special Education Tribunals*

These tribunals exist for parents dissatisfied with the decision of a Special Education Appeal Board.

The Tribunal's decision is final and binding.

Its powers are determined by the "Statutory Powers and Procedures Act" (a piece of provincial legislation).

The tribunal is also for parents who disagree with the outcome of the I.P.R.C. meeting of the school district.

Contact the tribunal at:
Ontario Special Education Tribunals
2 Bloor Street West, 24th Floor
Toronto ON M4W 3V5
Telephone: (416) 326-1116

## ALTERNATIVE SCHOOLING

### *Home Schooling*

The Board of Education must be advised by parents if they choose to educate their child at home in order to avoid truancy charges. A Board of Education cannot direct a parent to home school their child. The Board has a statutory obligation to ensure parents are providing a satisfactory education.

**Procedures for Parents**

Parents who decide to provide home schooling for their child(ren) should notify the school board of their intent in writing. Parents are required to provide the name, gender, and date of birth of each child who is receiving home schooling, and the telephone number and address of the home. The letter should be signed by the parent(s). If the home address changes, parents should notify the school board of the address change. If parents decide to continue to provide home schooling in subsequent years, they should give notification each year in writing prior to September 1 to the school board in whose jurisdiction their child last attended school. The letter should contain the same information as in the initial letter described above.

**Procedures for School Boards**

When parents give a board written notification of their intent to provide home schooling for their child, the board should consider the child to be excused from attendance at school, in accordance with subsection 21(2), clause (a), of the Education Act. The board should accept parents' written notification each year as evidence that the parents are providing satisfactory instruction at home. The board should send a letter each year to the parents, acknowledging the notification.

Normally, the board should not investigate the matter. However, if there are reasonable grounds to suspect the child is not receiving satisfactory instruction at home, the board should take steps to determine whether the instruction is satisfactory, as outlined in the next section.

## *Home Instruction*

If a student has medical evidence that they are unable to attend school the Board will usually provide between 4–8 hours per week of 1:1 instruction in the student's home or in the hospital. Medical documentation must be provided and each Board has their own policy on such matters.

## *Provincial and Demonstration Schools in Ontario*

The Ontario Ministry of Education is responsible for the administration of five sites with Provincial Schools for students who are Deaf, and one for students who are blind and/or deaf-blind and four Demonstration Schools (for students who have severe learning disabilities). The Provincial Schools Branch oversees the policies and operation of these schools. Qualified teachers employed by the Provincial Schools Authority or seconded from District School Boards deliver the educational programs.

Provincial Schools and Provincial Demonstration Schools:

- are operated by the Ministry of Education;
- provide education for students who are deaf or blind, or who have severe learning disabilities;
- provide an alternative education option;
- serve as regional resource centres for students who are deaf, blind, or deaf-blind;
- provide preschool home visiting services for students who are deaf or deaf-blind;
- develop and provide learning materials and media for students who are deaf, blind, or deaf-blind;
- provide school board teachers with resource services;
- play a valuable role in teacher training.

Provincial and Demonstration Schools were established to:

- Provide special residential education programs for students between the ages of 5 and 21 years;
- Enhance the development of each student's academic and social skills;
- Develop abilities of students enrolled to a level that will enable them to return to programs operated by a local school board within two years.

In addition to providing residential schooling to students with severe learning disabilities, the provincial Demonstration schools have special programs for students with severe learning disabilities in association with attention-deficit/hyperactivity disorder (ADD/ADHD). These are highly intensive one-year programs.

**Examples**

> W. Ross Macdonald School – School for the Deaf and Deaf-Blind, Brantford, Ontario
> The Ernest C. Drury School for the Deaf, Milton, Ontario
> Amethyst School – For Children with Severe Learning Disabilities, London, Ontario

**For more information visit:** http://www.psbnet.ca/eng/schools/index.html

## *Child Advocacy Program*

The CAP Education Law Program is a free legal service available to low- and moderate-income families whose children face challenges to their rights at school. Lawyers help students and their parents understand their legal rights and negotiate solutions when they feel unable to resolve conflicts with school administrators and officials. This service helps safeguard the public education rights of children and youth across Ontario and ensure due process in education legal matters.

The volunteer lawyers who take CAP cases are experienced and trained in Education Law and provide free legal services to:

- Students who have trouble accessing Special Education services;
- Children and youth who face suspension, expulsion, or exclusion;
- Children and youth being denied the right to attend school;
- Bullying, harassment, and school safety issues.

CAP lawyers can help in three ways:

- By consulting with students and families on their legal rights;
- By intervening on behalf of students with school administrators (by letter, phone, or in person);
- By representing students at tribunals or hearings.

**For more information visit**: http://www.childadvocacy.ca/

### Roles of a CYW in the School System

1. assigned to one school and serve the general population;
2. assigned to one school but work with particular students designated by the principal;
3. assigned to several schools as a resource consultant;
4. section 23 classroom – on or off school property;
5. assigned to a single special education class in a single school.

## EDUCATION LINKS AND REFERENCES

*Child Advocacy Project*. http://www.childadvocacy.ca/

Justice for Children and Youth. *Physical Punishment Pamphlet*.
       http://www.cleonet.ca/instance.php?instance_id=2458

ONIP Online. *Understanding the Education System in Ontario*
       http://www.onip.ca/article/25

Ontario Ministry of Education. http://www.edu.gov.on.ca/

Ontario Ministry of Education. (2009). Keeping our Kids Safe at School: Reporting and Respond-
       ing to Incidents. http://www.edu.gov.on.ca/eng/safeschools/KeepKidSafeSchool.pdf

Ontario Ministry of Education. (2009). Suspensions and Expulsions: What Parents Need
       to Know. http://www.edu.gov.on.ca/eng/safeschools/NeedtoKnowSExp.pdf

Ontario Ministry of Education. *Special Education*
       http://www.edu.gov.on.ca/eng/general/elemsec/speced/speced.html

Provincial Ministry of Education. *Our Provincial and Demonstration Schools*.
       http://www.psbnet.ca/eng/schools/index.html

*TCDSB Section 23 Overview*. http://www.tcdsb.org/section23/Overview.htm

# APPENDICES

# THE BROADER CONTEXT OF PARLIAMENT

Parliament as a legislative body functions as an instrument of government within a broader structure that includes the Executive Branch and the Judicial Branch.

In the Westminster-based model of parliamentary government, the Executive, composed of the Prime Minister and the Cabinet, is incorporated into Parliament, while retaining a separate sphere of authority and autonomy. The Judiciary, consisting of the Supreme Court and all the other courts of the land, is the third branch of government that is also independent of either Parliament or the Executive.

## Canada's Parliamentary System

| EXECUTIVE BRANCH | QUEEN Represented in Canada By Governor General | LEGISLATIVE BRANCH |
|---|---|---|
|  | SENATE 105 members appointed by Prime Minister who may serve up to age of 75 |  |
| PRIME MINISTER AND CABINET | HOUSE OF COMMONS 301 members elected for up to 5 years |  |

JUDICIAL BRANCH

SUPREME COURT OF CANADA

FEDERAL COURT OF CANADA      SUPERIOR COURTS in the provinces

Source: Government of Canada. (2002), "Inside Canada's Parliament." Library of Parliament. [Online]. Available: http://www.parl.gc.ca/Information/library/inside/index-e.htm

# COMMUNITY RESOURCES AND LEGISLATION

**For more information, see** Eugene Forsey, *How Canadians Govern Themselves* at

http://www.parl.gc.ca/about/parliament/senatoreugeneforsey/book/preface-e.html

# KIDS HELP PHONE

For more information, see http://org.kidshelpphone.ca or call 1-800-668-6868.

# LINKS

- **Child Welfare League of Canada** www.cwlc.ca
- **Child Welfare Resource Centre** (links in child welfare) www.childwelfare.ca
- **Children's Aid Foundation** www.cafdn.org
- **Foster Parent's Society of Ontario** www.fosterparentssociety.org
- **Ontario Association of Children's Aid Societies** www.oacas.org

For more about the Canadian national association for CYCs, and CYC associations in other provinces, visit the **Council of Canadian Child and Youth Care Associations (CCCYCA)** site at: www.cyccanada.ca.

# THE OFFICE OF THE CHILDREN'S LAWYER

The Office of the Children's Lawyer is a law office in the Ministry of the Attorney General that delivers programs in the administration of justice on behalf of children under the age of 18 with respect to their personal and property rights. Lawyers within the office represent children in various areas of law including child custody and access disputes, child protection proceedings, estate matters, and civil litigation. Clinical investigators prepare reports for the court in custody/access proceedings and may assist lawyers who are representing children in such matters.

The origin of the Office of the Children's Lawyer in Ontario can be traced back to as early as 1826 when the Lord Chancellor of Upper Canada appointed a leading member of the legal bar to be guardian ad litem of minors (persons under the age of 18 years) when they were being sued and to represent their interests in court.

Lucy McSweeney is the current Children's Lawyer for Ontario.

**Contact Information:**
14th Floor
393 University Avenue
Toronto ON M5G 1W9

Tel: (416) 314-8000
Fax: (416) 314-8050

# THE OFFICE OF OMBUDSMAN

THE OFFICE OF OMBUDSMAN was established by the Ontario legislature in 1975. Arthur Maloney was sworn in as the province's first Ombudsman in October of that year, following passage of the Ombudsman Act. In October 2000, Ombudsman Ontario celebrated its 25th anniversary. The current Ombudsman is Andre Marin.

The Ombudsman's job is to investigate complaints about provincial government organizations. When he finds something wrong he can make recommendations to resolve the problem, and if these are not acted upon, he can report the case to the Legislature. The Ombudsman can also help resolve complaints informally. Ontario's Ombudsman is an Officer of the provincial Legislature who is independent of the government and political parties.

Some examples of complaints that may be investigated:

- disability benefits
- workplace safety and insurance
- Family Responsibility Office
- treatment of inmates
- patient care in provincial psychiatric hospitals

The Ombudsman's work is confidential and free.

*http://www.ombudsman.on.ca/*

**Access Centre**
1-800-263-1830 - English
1-800-387-2620 - French
1-866-411-4211 - TTY, hard of hearing and deaf
416-586-3300 - Toronto
416-586-3485 - Toronto Fax

**Note:** In the past few years, the Office of the Ombudsman has been forced to close several of its regional offices (four out of ten offices closed in 2000). In addition to these closures some materials are not readily available. For example, the blue self-addressed, stamped forms and envelopes for youth to submit anonymously is in short supply.

*Source: Office of The Ombudsman. (2004, September 24). "Who We Are." "What We Do." "Contact." http://www.ombudsman. on.ca/*

# OFFICE OF THE PROVINCIAL ADVOCATE FOR CHILDREN AND YOUTH

**For more information, see** http://provincialadvocate.on.ca or call 1-800-263-2841.

# DUTY TO REPORT

## Duty to report child in need of protection

72. (1) Despite the provisions of any other Act, if a person, including a person who performs professional or official duties with respect to children, has reasonable grounds to suspect one of the following, the person shall forthwith report the suspicion and the information on which it is based to a society:

1. The child has suffered physical harm, inflicted by the person having charge of the child or caused by or resulting from that person's,
   i. failure to adequately care for, provide for, supervise or protect the child, or
   ii. pattern of neglect in caring for, providing for, supervising or protecting the child.
2. There is a risk that the child is likely to suffer physical harm inflicted by the person having charge of the child or caused by or resulting from that person's,
   i. failure to adequately care for, provide for, supervise or protect the child, or
   ii. pattern of neglect in caring for, providing for, supervising or protecting the child.
3. The child has been sexually molested or sexually exploited, by the person having charge of the child or by another person where the person having charge of the child knows or should know of the possibility of sexual molestation or sexual exploitation and fails to protect the child.
4. There is a risk that the child is likely to be sexually molested or sexually exploited as described in paragraph 3.
5. The child requires medical treatment to cure, prevent or alleviate physical harm or suffering and the child's parent or the person having charge of the child does not provide, or refuses or is unavailable or unable to consent to, the treatment.
6. The child has suffered emotional harm, demonstrated by serious,
   i. anxiety,
   ii. depression,
   iii. withdrawal,
   iv. self-destructive or aggressive behaviour, or
   v. delayed development,
   and there are reasonable grounds to believe that the emotional harm suffered by the child results from the actions, failure to act or pattern of neglect on the part of the child's parent or the person having charge of the child.
7. The child has suffered emotional harm of the kind described in subparagraph i, ii, iii, iv or v of paragraph 6 and the child's parent or the person having charge of the child does not provide, or refuses or is unavailable or unable to consent to, services or treatment to remedy or alleviate the harm.

8. There is a risk that the child is likely to suffer emotional harm of the kind described in sub-paragraph i, ii, iii, iv or v of paragraph 6 resulting from the actions, failure to act or pattern of neglect on the part of the child's parent or the person having charge of the child.

9. There is a risk that the child is likely to suffer emotional harm of the kind described in subparagraph i, ii, iii, iv or v of paragraph 6 and that the child's parent or the person having charge of the child does not provide, or refuses or is unavailable or unable to consent to, services or treatment to prevent the harm.

10. The child suffers from a mental, emotional or developmental condition that, if not remedied, could seriously impair the child's development and the child's parent or the person having charge of the child does not provide, or refuses or is unavailable or unable to consent to, treatment to remedy or alleviate the condition.

11. The child has been abandoned, the child's parent has died or is unavailable to exercise his or her custodial rights over the child and has not made adequate provision for the child's care and custody, or the child is in a residential placement and the parent refuses or is unable or unwilling to resume the child's care and custody.

12. The child is less than 12 years old and has killed or seriously injured another person or caused serious damage to another person's property, services or treatment are necessary to prevent a recurrence and the child's parent or the person having charge of the child does not provide, or refuses or is unavailable or unable to consent to, those services or treatment.

13. The child is less than 12 years old and has on more than one occasion injured another person or caused loss or damage to another person's property, with the encouragement of the person having charge of the child or because of that person's failure or inability to supervise the child adequately. 1999, c. 2, s. 22 (1).

# ONGOING DUTY TO REPORT

(2) A person who has additional reasonable grounds to suspect one of the matters set out in subsection (1) shall make a further report under subsection (1) even if he or she has made previous reports with respect to the same child. 1999, c. 2, s. 22 (1).

# PERSON MUST REPORT DIRECTLY

(3) A person who has a duty to report a matter under subsection (1) or (2) shall make the report directly to the society and shall not rely on any other person to report on his or her behalf. 1999, c. 2, s. 22 (1).

# OFFENCE

(4) A person referred to in subsection (5) is guilty of an offence if,

    (a)   he or she contravenes subsection (1) or (2) by not reporting a suspicion; and

    (b)   the information on which it was based was obtained in the course of his or her professional or official duties. 1999, c. 2, s. 22 (2).

# SAME

(5) Subsection (4) applies to every person who performs professional or official duties with respect to children including,

    (a)   a health care professional, including a physician, nurse, dentist, pharmacist and psychologist;

    (b)   a teacher, school principal, social worker, family counsellor, priest, rabbi, member of the clergy, operator or employee of a day nursery and youth and recreation worker;

    (c)   a peace officer and a coroner;

    (d)   a solicitor; and

    (e)   a service provider and an employee of a service provider. 1999, c. 2, s. 22 (3).

# SAME

(6) In clause (5) (b),

"youth and recreation worker" does not include a volunteer. 1999, c. 2, s. 22 (3).

# SAME

(6.1) A director, officer or employee of a corporation who authorizes, permits or concurs in a contravention of an offence under subsection (4) by an employee of the corporation is guilty of an offence. 1999, c. 2, s. 22 (3).

# SAME

(6.2) A person convicted of an offence under subsection (4) or (6.1) is liable to a fine of not more than $1,000. 1999, c. 2, s. 22 (3).

# SECTION OVERRIDES PRIVILEGE

(7) This section applies although the information reported may be confidential or privileged, and no action for making the report shall be instituted against a person who acts in accordance with this section unless the person acts maliciously or without reasonable grounds for the suspicion. R.S.O. 1990, c. C.11, s. 72 (7); 1999, c. 2, s. 22 (4).

# EXCEPTION: SOLICITOR CLIENT PRIVILEGE

(8) Nothing in this section abrogates any privilege that may exist between a solicitor and his or her client. R.S.O. 1990, c. C.11, s. 72 (8).

Note: Effective November 1, 2004, Section 72 is amended by the Statutes of Ontario, 2004, chapter 3, Schedule A, subsection 78 (2) by the addition of the following subsection:

Conflict

(9) This section prevails despite anything in the Personal Health Information Protection Act, 2004. 2004, c. 3, Sched. A, s. 78 (2).

See: 2004, c. 3, Sched. A, ss. 78 (2), 99 (2).

*Source: Child and Family Services Act, Revised Statutes of Ontario, 1990, Chapter C.11*

# PARAMOUNT PURPOSE AND OTHER PURPOSES

## PARAMOUNT PURPOSE

1. (1) The paramount purpose of this Act is to promote the best interests, protection and well being of children.

(2) The additional purposes of this Act, so long as they are consistent with the best interests, protection and well being of children, are:

1. To recognize that while parents may need help in caring for their children, that help should give support to the autonomy and integrity of the family unit and, wherever possible, be provided on the basis of mutual consent.
2. To recognize that the least disruptive course of action that is available and is appropriate in a particular case to help a child should be considered.
3. To recognize that children's services should be provided in a manner that,
   i.  respects children's needs for continuity of care and for stable family relationships, and
   ii. takes into account physical and mental developmental differences among children.
4. To recognize that, wherever possible, services to children and their families should be provided in a manner that respects cultural, religious and regional differences.
5. To recognize that Indian and native people should be entitled to provide, wherever possible, their own child and family services, and that all services to Indian and native children and families should be provided in a manner that recognizes their culture, heritage and traditions and the concept of the extended family.  1999, c. 2, s. 1.

*Source: Child and Family Services Act, Revised Statutes of Ontario, 1990, Chapter C.11*

# DECLARATION OF PRINCIPLE/*YCJA*

3. (1) The following principles apply in this Act:

(a) the youth criminal justice system is intended to

- (i) prevent crime by addressing the circumstances underlying a young person's offending behaviour,
- (ii) rehabilitate young persons who commit offences and reintegrate them into society, and
- (iii) ensure that a young person is subject to meaningful consequences for his or her offence in order to promote the long-term protection of the public;

(b) the criminal justice system for young persons must be separate from that of adults and emphasize the following:

- (i) rehabilitation and reintegration,
- (ii) fair and proportionate accountability that is consistent with the greater dependency of young persons and their reduced level of maturity,
- (iii) enhanced procedural protection to ensure that young persons are treated fairly and that their rights, including their right to privacy, are protected,
- (iv) timely intervention that reinforces the link between the offending behaviour and its consequences, and
- (v) the promptness and speed with which persons responsible for enforcing this Act must act, given young persons' perception of time;

(c) within the limits of fair and proportionate accountability, the measures taken against young persons who commit offences should

- (i) reinforce respect for societal values,
- (ii) encourage the repair of harm done to victims and the community,
- (iii) be meaningful for the individual young person given his or her needs and level of development and, where appropriate, involve the parents, the extended family, the community and social or other agencies in the young person's rehabilitation and reintegration, and
- (iv) respect gender, ethnic, cultural and linguistic differences and respond to the needs of aboriginal young persons and of young persons with special requirements; and

(d) special considerations apply in respect of proceedings against young persons and, in particular,

- (i) young persons have rights and freedoms in their own right, such as a right to be heard in the course of and to participate in the processes, other than the decision to prosecute, that lead to decisions that affect them, and young persons have special guarantees of their rights and freedoms,
- (ii) victims should be treated with courtesy, compassion and respect for their dignity and privacy and should suffer the minimum degree of inconvenience as a result of their involvement with the youth criminal justice system,

(iii)   victims should be provided with information about the proceedings and given an opportunity to participate and be heard, and

(iv)   Parents should be informed of measures or proceedings involving their children and encouraged to support them in addressing their offending behaviour.

*Source: Department of Justice Canada. (2002, September). YCJA Explained. (CD-ROM). Explanatory Materials. Youth Criminal Justice Act.*

# EXTRA JUDICIAL MEASURES, SANCTIONS AND SENTENCING OPTIONS

The following extrajudicial measures may be used by the Police:

- take no further action;
- give the young person an informal warning;
- give the young person a formal police caution;
- refer the young person to a community program or agency to assist the young person in not committing offences; or
- refer the young person to an extrajudicial sanctions program.

The Act identifies the following extrajudicial measures that may be used by the Crown attorney:

- give the young person a Crown caution; or
- refer the young person to an extrajudicial sanctions program.

Of course, the Crown may also decide not to proceed with the charge and may refer the young person to a community program or agency to assist the young person in not committing offences.

Section 19 of the Act authorizes a police officer or a Crown attorney to convene or cause to be convened a conference in order to obtain advice on appropriate extrajudicial measures. Conferences provide an opportunity for a wide range of perspectives on a case, more creative solutions, better coordination of services, and increased involvement of the victim and other community members in the youth justice system.

A conference could be composed of a variety of people depending on the situation. It could include, for example, the parents of the young person, the victim, others who are familiar with the young person and his or her neighborhood, representatives of community agencies or professionals with a particular expertise that may be needed.

A conference could be a restorative mechanism that is focused on developing a proposal for an extrajudicial sanction involving the young person in repairing the harm done to the victim of the offence. Such a proposal would be advice to a police officer or Crown attorney who would make the decision on the appropriate sanction, taking into account the relevant provisions of the Act. A conference could also be a professional case conference in which professionals provide advice on how services in the community can be coordinated to assist the young person.

## TAKING NO FURTHER ACTION

For many minor offences, a decision by the police officer to take no further action may be the most sensible thing to do. For example, the parents of the young person, the victim or others may have already taken sufficient steps to hold the young person accountable. There would be no need to expend limited police resources and other youth justice system resources on such a case.

## WARNING THE YOUNG PERSON

Warnings by police officers under Section 6 are intended to be informal warnings. They are an example of a traditional exercise of police discretion. Experience under the *YOA* has caused concern that police have decreased their use of this type of informal police discretion and replaced it with charges or referrals to an alternative measures program.

In many minor cases, a warning by a police officer is a sufficient response from the justice system, just as it was for the parents and grandparents of today's youth. It lets a youth know the limits of acceptable behavior. There is also evidence that, in terms of recidivism, a warning or taking no further action is as effective as charging the youth or referring him or her to an alternative measures program.

## POLICE CAUTION

Police cautions are more formal warnings by the police. Based on the experience in some jurisdictions, it is expected that a police caution will be in the form of a letter from the police to the young person and the parents, or it may involve a process in which the young person and the parents are requested to appear at a police station to talk to a senior police officer about the alleged offence.

A police caution is intended to make clear to the young person the seriousness of the alleged offence and to provide a police response that is between an informal warning and a charge. As with all extrajudicial measures, a police caution may only be used if the police officer has reasonable grounds to charge the young person with an offence. Also, the caution should not be used in cases in which taking no further action or an informal warning would be sufficient.

- Cautioning is an increasingly important way of avoiding court proceedings and reducing, for many offenders, the risk of recidivism.
- "Net widening" is a danger to be avoided.
- Taking no further action or using informal warnings instead of formal cautions is to be encouraged.
- If the offence is not serious, prosecution is, in general, not justifiable (a serious offence is determined by "whether significant harm has been done to a person, substantial damage has been done or property of substantial value has been stolen").
- Second and subsequent cautions should not be precluded when (a) there was a reasonable lapse of time between offences, or (b) the earlier offence was trivial or different in character.

- There is an advantage in the police seeking the views of other agencies where the police decision is not obvious.

Although Section 7 of the *YCJA* authorizes provinces to establish a police caution program, provinces are not required to do so. However, the terms "police caution" and "warning" are not defined in the Act and the giving of warnings under the Act is not dependent on a province establishing a program. Police may be able to achieve the benefits of formal cautions through effective policies and guidelines on warnings.

## REFERRALS TO COMMUNITY PROGRAMS

Police officers may, instead of charging a young person, refer the young person to a community program or agency that may help him or her not to commit offences. The consent of the young person is required. The referral may be to a wide range of community resources, including recreation programs, counseling agencies, child welfare agencies and mental health programs.

The purpose of the referral is to connect the young person to a program or agency that may address factors that seem to be related to the young person's involvement in crime.

It is important to recognize that a young person may feel intimidated when dealing with a police officer and may feel coerced into agreeing to a referral to a community program or agency. The requirement that the referral can be made only with the consent of the young person means that the consent must be informed and voluntary. The young person should be advised of the right to counsel and be given a reasonable opportunity to consult with counsel.

## CROWN CAUTIONS

Section 8 authorizes the Attorney General to establish a Crown cautioning program in a jurisdiction. This would permit prosecutors to give a caution to a young person instead of using the court process or extrajudicial sanctions. As with police cautioning, each jurisdiction will determine whether Crown cautions will be available and, if so, the form they will take.

Crown cautions are similar to police cautions but prosecutors give the caution after the police refer the case to them. In one province where they are currently being used, the caution is in the form of a letter to the young person and the parents.

## EXTRAJUDICIAL SANCTIONS

Extrajudicial sanctions, known as alternative measures under the *YOA*, are a type of extrajudicial measure that is intended for more serious offences and offenders than would be dealt with by warnings, cautions, and referrals. In comparison to other types of extrajudicial measures, a more formal set of rules applies to extrajudicial sanctions. Extrajudicial sanctions may be used only if:

- **Other extrajudicial measures would not be adequate**. Section 10 of the Act provides that an extrajudicial sanction may be used only if the young person cannot be adequately dealt with by another type of extrajudicial measure: an informal warning, a police caution, Crown caution or referral to a community program.

  There is evidence that under the YOA alternative measures programs have been used primarily for first-time offenders who have committed very minor offences. Some of the less serious cases that are currently being dealt with by alternative measures can be dealt with by warnings, cautions, and referrals, thus enabling extrajudicial sanctions to be used with cases that would otherwise be sent to the youth court. This approach encourages an increased use of extrajudicial measures that will allow the youth court to be focused on more serious cases.

The fact that an extrajudicial sanction has been used with respect to a young person who is alleged to have committed an offence does not take away the power to lay a charge or to proceed with a prosecution. The court has the power, however, to dismiss the charge in such cases. Where a charge is laid against the young person in respect of an offence, the court must dismiss the charge if it believes that the young person has totally complied with the terms of the extrajudicial sanction. If the court finds only partial compliance has occurred, it may still dismiss the charge if it believes a prosecution would be unfair. Evidence that a young person has been dealt with by a warning, caution, or referral is inadmissible in any court proceedings for the purpose of proving prior offending behavior. Unlike extrajudicial sanctions, the use of one of these other extrajudicial measures does not require a finding of guilt or an admission of responsibility by the young person. In such cases it would be unfair to use such evidence against the young person to, for example, increase the severity of a sentence for a subsequent offence.

In contrast, evidence that a young person has been dealt with previously by an extrajudicial sanction can be used at sentencing for a subsequent offence. Section 40 requires that a pre-sentence report include the history of extrajudicial sanctions used to deal with the young person and the response of the young person to those sanctions. Subsection 119(2) limits access to a record of extrajudicial sanctions to two years and possibly longer.

## YOUTH SENTENCING OPTIONS

There is a broad range of possible sanctions that a court may consider in determining an appropriate sentence. A sentence must be in accordance with the purpose and principles of sentencing and may consist of one or more sanctions that are not inconsistent with each other. These various sanctions or sentencing options include several new options along with options that existed under the *YOA*.

The options include both non-custodial and custodial sentences. All custodial sentences include a portion that the young person is to serve under supervision in the community. Before imposing a sentence that involves custody, the court must satisfy itself that none of the restrictions on custody set out in the *YCJA* exist.

# NON-CUSTODIAL SENTENCING OPTIONS

The majority of sentencing options provide alternatives to custody, consistent with the objective in the preamble to the *YCJA* of reducing the over-reliance on incarceration for non-violent young persons. The *YCJA* provides a range of alternatives that allow a sentencing response to be tailored to the individual case, including several new options.

## *Reprimand*

This **new** sentencing option is a formal rebuke by the judge in court. It is essentially a stern scolding or lecture from the judge and may be most appropriate in minor cases in which the experience of being apprehended, taken through the court process and reprimanded appears to be sufficient to hold the young person accountable for the offence. It can reinforce to the young person that his or her *behavior* was wrong. It may be appropriate in cases in which the court has determined that reparation made by the offender to the victim, or time spent by the offender in detention, essentially satisfies the requirement of a proportionate sentence. A reprimand may also serve as a means of communicating to the prosecutor that, in the court's opinion, the case should have been dealt with outside the court process. The period of access to the record of a reprimand is two months This period is much shorter than the period of access that applies to the record of an absolute discharge (two years) or a conditional discharge (three years).

## *Absolute Discharge*

The court may order an absolute discharge of the young person if it is in the best interests of the youth and not contrary to the public interest.

## *Conditional Discharge*

The court may order a discharge of the young person on conditions. In addition, the court may require the young person to report to and be supervised by the provincial director.

## Fine

The court may impose a fine up to $1000 on the young person. The court must consider the youth's ability to pay but has discretion in fixing time and terms for payment. Provinces may establish work programs for young persons to earn work credits toward paying the fine. A surcharge may be imposed on the fine and used, at the province's discretion, to provide assistance to victims' services.

## Compensation

The court may order a young person to compensate another person for loss, damage, or injury, by paying an amount of money determined by the court. The court must consider the youth's ability to pay and has discretion in fixing the time and terms for payment. As with all of the sentencing options, the court must comply with the purpose and principles of sentencing in imposing this sanction. The principle of proportionality, for example, may restrict the amount of compensation that may be ordered. The amount of loss or damage caused by the offence may exceed the seriousness of the offence and the degree of responsibility of the young person. As discussed above, a relevant factor in determining the seriousness of the case and, therefore, a proportionate sentence is whether the loss or damage was intended or could reasonably have been foreseen by the young person. In addition, accountability of young persons must be consistent with their greater dependency and reduced level of maturity.

## Restitution

The court may order restitution of property to the person owning it at the time of the offence.

## Reimbursement of Innocent Purchaser

If the court has ordered restitution of property to its owner, the court may also order the reimbursement of an innocent purchaser of the property. The court may fix the time and terms for payment. As noted above with respect to compensation orders, the amount of money that the court may order as reimbursement is subject to the sentencing principles, including the principle of proportionality.

## Personal Service

The court may order the young person to compensate a person by way of personal service for a loss, damage, or injury suffered. Alternatively, the court may order that the compensation be in kind. An order under paragraph 42(2) (h) requires the consent of the person to be compensated. In addition, the order must not interfere with the young person's normal hours of education or work. The order must not exceed 240 hours of service that can be completed within 12 months.

## Community Service

The court may order a young person to perform community service that does not exceed 240 hours of service that can be completed within 12 months. The community service must be part of a program approved by the provincial director or the person or organization for which the service is to be performed must have consented to it.

## Prohibition Order

The court may impose on the young person an order of prohibition, seizure, or forfeiture that is authorized under federal legislation. If a young person is found guilty of an offence referred to in subsection 109(1) of the *Criminal Code* (e.g., an indictable offence in which violence was used and is punishable by imprisonment for ten years or more), the court must make an order prohibiting the young person from possessing a firearm, cross-bow, prohibited weapon, restricted weapon, prohibited device, ammunition, prohibited ammunition or explosive substance. This mandatory prohibition order ends not earlier than two years after the completion of the custodial portion of the sentence or, in the case of a non-custodial sentence, after the finding of guilt.

## Probation

The young person may be placed on probation, with conditions, for a period of up to two years. Section 55 sets out mandatory and optional conditions of probation orders. The potential range of conditions is very broad. The conditions may include requiring the young person to attend school, reside in a place that the provincial director may specify, and "any other conditions" that the court considers appropriate. Although the flexibility of a probation order permits creative, individualized sentences, it must be used with restraint because of the negative consequences of imposing unrealistic and "over-reaching" or intrusive conditions on a young person for a period of up to two years.

A serious concern in the setting of probation conditions for a young person is that the conditions may set up the young person for failure and, therefore, a possible charge of breach of probation. The result may be that a young person is incarcerated for behavior that would not justify a criminal charge if it were not related to a probation order.

Conditions of probation must be assessed as to whether or not they are in accordance with the purpose and principles of sentencing.

## Intensive Support and Supervision Program Order

In this new sentencing option, the young person receives a high level of support and supervision in the community to assist him or her to change his or her behavior. It is intended to provide closer monitoring and more support than probation. It is intended to provide much smaller caseloads than probation and is particularly well-suited for many offenders who under the *YOA* have been sentenced to custody.

The support for the youth should be designed to respond to the specific needs or problems that appear to contribute to the youth's offending behavior. Since the youths who are subject to this order are likely to have significant and multiple needs, the provincial program to implement the order should have sufficient flexibility to allow the support to be individualized and targeted to those specific needs.

## *Attendance Order*

This **new** sentencing option requires the young person to attend a program at specified times (up to a maximum of 240 hours over a six-month period) and to abide by conditions set by the judge. It is a nonresidential program that, for many offenders, can provide an alternative to a custodial sentence. It can be designed to address the particular circumstances of the young person. For example, it could be focused on specific times and days when a young person is unsupervised and tends to violate the law. As with intensive support and supervision programs, federal-provincial cost sharing agreements for the *YCJA*'s implementation specifically identify attendance programs as one of the high priority areas in which provinces are able to receive additional federal funding.

# CUSTODIAL SENTENCING OPTIONS

The *YCJA* clearly reflects a strong preference for non-custodial sentences wherever possible. The preamble to the *YCJA* states that the youth justice system should reserve its most serious intervention for the most serious crimes and reduce the over-reliance on incarceration for nonviolent young persons. Sentencing principles emphasize the requirement of proportionality in sentencing and, within the limits of proportionality, the requirements of the least restrictive alternative and the promotion of rehabilitation and reintegration. The restrictions on custody in Section 39 prohibit custody in many cases and require a thorough exploration of alternatives to custody in cases in which custody is not prohibited. If the court decides to impose custody, the court must justify its decision by including in its reasons for decision and explanation of why a non-custodial sentence was not adequate to hold the young person accountable.

These are the sentencing options in the *YCJA* that allow the court to impose a sentence that includes custody:

## Deferred Custody and Supervision

If a young person is found guilty of an offence that is not a serious violent offence, the court may impose the **new** sentencing option of deferred custody and supervision if it is consistent with the purpose and principles of sentencing and the restrictions on custody in Section 39 (ss. 42(2)-(5)). Although the young person serves the sentence in the community on conditions, it should be considered, for most purposes, a type of custodial sentence because a breach of a condition can result in the young person serving the remainder of the sentence as a custody and supervision order.

A deferred custody and supervision order may be for a specified period that is less than six months. During that time, the young person is in the community and must follow conditions set by the youth justice court judge. A breach of conditions may result in a modification of the conditions. It is also possible for a young person who breaches the conditions to be ordered to serve the remaining time as a custody and supervision order.

## Custody and Supervision Orders

Unlike the *YOA*, the *YCJA* provides that all custody orders include a period of supervision in the community. The purpose of the community supervision portion is to ensure appropriate supervision and support for the young person during the transition from custody back to his or her community.

The *YCJA* contains a list of mandatory conditions that apply to all young persons while under supervision in the community. Additional conditions can be imposed to support the young person and address his or her needs, as well as manage risk. If a young person breaches a condition while under supervision in the community, reviews will be held that can result in a change in conditions or in the young person being returned to custody.

It is also possible that a young person may not serve a portion of the sentence in the community following custody. Before the start of the community portion, the court can require the young person to remain in custody if the court is satisfied that there are reasonable grounds to believe that a young person will commit an offence causing death or serious harm before the end of the sentence.

The possible overall length of custody and supervision orders, the possible length of the community portion of the order, and the enforcement procedure in the event of a breach vary, depending on the offence.

## Most Offences

The maximum length of the custody and supervision order for most offences is two or three years, depending on the offence. The two-year maximum applies to all offences except offences for which an adult would be liable to life imprisonment. These latter offences, other than murder, can result in a maximum youth sentence of three years. The period of community supervision is one-half the length of the custody period

**Attempted murder, manslaughter, and aggravated sexual assault**: The maximum overall length of the custody and supervision order for the offences of attempted murder, manslaughter, and aggravated sexual assault is three years because these are offences for which an adult would be liable to life imprisonment.

The period of conditional supervision is set by the court and, therefore, is not necessarily one-half the length of the custody period. This provides the court added flexibility to tailor sentences imposed for these particularly serious offences. If the young person breaches a condition, the provincial director may bring the young person back into custody.

The court is not required to impose a sentence for these offences. The court may decide to impose any other sentence under subsection 42(2) of the Act.

**Murder:** The offence of murder is the only offence under the YCJA that must result in a custody and supervision order. The maximum length of the order is ten years for first-degree murder and seven years for second-degree murder. As with other presumptive offences, the period of conditional supervision is set by the court and, therefore, is not necessarily one-half the length of the custody period.

## Open Custody

The custodial part of the youth's disposition takes place in a group home like setting in the community. Open custody facilities are staffed by child and youth workers and correctional service workers. Youth are monitored closely and there exists a high level of accountability. Community access is closely monitored, often supervised and frequently restricted to staff escorted movement within the community. The community supervision portion of the disposition is half the length of the custodial disposition. Example: Six months open custody followed by three months community supervision followed by one year probation.

## Closed Custody or Secure Custody

Secure custody is defined as "a place or facility designated by the Lieutenant Governor-in-Council ... for the secure containment or restraint of young persons." Secure custody is often

called closed custody. Access to the community is limited or non-existent. Secure custody facilities are often called youth jails. The community supervision portion of the disposition is half the length of the custodial disposition. Example: Six months secure custody followed by three months community supervision followed by one year probation. Sometimes a disposition of open custody follows a secure custody disposition. This can happen at sentencing or via a youth court review presided over by the original sentencing judge.

## Intensive Rehabilitative Custody and Supervision Order

The intensive rehabilitative custody and supervision order is a **new** special youth sentence intended to provide treatment for serious violent offenders. The order may be made if the court determines that the following criteria are met:

- the young person has been found guilty of murder, attempted murder, manslaughter, aggravated sexual assault, or a third serious violent offence
- the young person is suffering from a mental or psychological disorder
- an individualized treatment plan for the young person has been developed and
- the provincial director has determined that an intensive rehabilitative custody and supervision program is available and the young person's participation is appropriate

Special federal funding for provinces and territories has been set aside to ensure that this sentencing option can be available throughout the country. This special treatment sentence offers a significant new option in the youth justice system for serious violent young offenders who otherwise might receive an adult sentence. This order is not available if an adult sentence is ordered. The order is not limited to young persons who are 14 to 17 years of age. The court may order a 12- or 13-year-old into intensive rehabilitative custody and supervision.

The young person's right to consent to or refuse such treatment under common law or provincial legislation must be respected.

# LEARNING DISABILITIES: A NEW DEFINITION

"Learning Disabilities" refers to a variety of disorders that affect the acquisition, retention, understanding, organization, or use of verbal and/or non-verbal information. These disorders result from impairments in one or more psychological processes related to learning, in combination with otherwise average abilities essential for thinking and reasoning. Learning disabilities are specific not global impairments and as such are distinct from intellectual disabilities.

Learning disabilities range in severity and invariably interfere with the acquisition and use of one or more of the following important skills:

- oral language (e.g., listening, speaking, understanding)
- reading (e.g., decoding, comprehension)
- written language (e.g., spelling, written expression)
- mathematics (e.g., computation, problem solving)

Learning disabilities may also cause difficulties with organizational skills, social perception, and social interaction.

The impairments are generally life-long. However, their effects may be expressed differently over time, depending on the match between the demands of the environment and the individual's characteristics. Some impairment may be noted during the pre-school years, while others may not become evident until much later. During the school years, learning disabilities are suggested by unexpectedly low academic achievement or achievement that is sustainable only by extremely high levels of effort and support.

Learning disabilities are due to genetic, other congenital, and/or acquired neuro-biological factors. They are not caused by factors such as cultural or language differences, inadequate or inappropriate instruction, socio-economic status or lack of motivation, although any one of these and other factors may compound the impact of learning disabilities. Frequently learning disabilities co-exist with other conditions, including attentional, behavioural and emotional disorders, sensory impairments, or other medical conditions.

For success, persons with learning disabilities require specialized interventions in home, school, community and workplace settings, appropriate to their individual strengths and needs, including:

- specific skill instruction;
- the development of compensatory strategies;
- the development of self-advocacy skills;
- appropriate accommodations.

The term **"psychological processes"** describes an evolving list of cognitive functions. To date, research has focused on functions such as:

- phonological processing;
- memory and attention;
- processing speed;
- language processing;
- perceptual-motor processing;
- visual-spatial processing;
- executive functions; (e.g., planning, monitoring and metacognitive abilities).

This definition is supported by a background document entitled: *Operationalizing the New Definition of Learning Disabilities for Utilization within Ontario's Educational System*, LDAO, 2001.